CREATIVE STRATEGIES for
SCHOOL PROBLEMS

Michael Durrant

Eastwood Family Therapy Centre
Epping, NSW, Australia

Printed and published in Australia

Typesetting and design by Eastwood Family Therapy Centre.
Printed and bound by Bell Graphics, Alexandria, NSW.

ISBN 0 646 14935 0

Eastwood Family Therapy Centre
Michael Durrant & Associates Pty Ltd
P.O. Box 630, Epping, NSW, AUSTRALIA 2121
Phone: (02) 868 2799   Fax: (02) 876 8943

Michael Durrant & Associates Pty Ltd
(ACN 002 821 409)

CONTENTS

CREATIVE STRATEGIES
for SCHOOL PROBLEMS ??

Over the last few years, I have had the opportunity to share ideas with school counsellors and teachers in a number of settings. I have met school personnel who find the demands and constraints of many approaches to therapy frustrating within the school setting. Most school counsellors and psychologists juggle two or three (or more) schools and simply do not have the luxury of sufficient time to undertake longterm therapy with students referred to them. Moreover, they find themselves asked for advice and consultation by teachers and principals, who do not want to allow time for "in-depth" assessment. The practical demands of the school situation mean that people are most concerned with finding what it is that *works*.

There is a story about Milton Erickson's approach to a boy who was failing to read.

An 11-year-old boy had failed to learn to read, despite the efforts of teachers, reading tutors, and so on. His parents, determined that he should read, tried to force him to learn and filled his summer vacation with remedial reading lessons. He was brought to Erickson, who agreed with him that his parents were wrong in thinking he could learn to read. "You know you can't read, and I know you can't read ... now what do you like doing?", Erickson is reported to have said. The boy began to describe his fishing trips with his father and the various different places around the country they had been fishing. During one discussion, Erickson asserted that it was a certain distance from the boy's home to one of the fishing spots and the boy contradicted him. Erickson produced a map and asked the boy to show him (and the boy was proved right). During a few sessions, Erickson and the boy talked about various fishing locations, and Erickson always looked in the wrong place on the map for them. The boy continued to correct him, finding and *reading* the names on the map. However, Erickson was clear that they were *looking at* the map, not *reading* it, and the boy gradually looked at more and more of the words on the map, continuing to prove Erickson's geography wrong. As their discussions proceeded, Erickson also made mistakes in talking about different types of fish, and the boy corrected him by looking at the descriptions in the encyclopaedia. Again, this was described as *looking*, not *reading*. Erickson suggested the boy and his father have a fishing trip during the coming vacation and the boy used various maps to plan the trip and, the following term, read an account of the trip to his teacher. (from Haley, 1973; O'Hanlon & Hexum, 1990)

Why did this work? Who knows! We can guess that the parents and boy (and teachers) had become locked in an escalating pattern of trying to *make* him learn to read and that, however much this seemed sensible, *it was simply not working*. Erickson's stance of agreeing with the boy and devoting the sessions to something else interrupted this pattern (as did spending the vacation fishing rather than being tutored). Or, perhaps it was just the accepting relationship with this "funny" old man that made a difference? Or, maybe it was that Erickson found a way to harness the boy's interests to encourage him, indirectly, to read? And, perhaps, the boy experienced himself reading voluntarily, and this changed his view of the situation?

Whatever it was, it worked.

Stewart and Nodrick (1990) describe their intervention in a case of a Year 4 boy, who had been assessed as having "learning disabilities" and who had experienced a cycle of failure and frustration.

After talking with the boy (and his family) about the extent to which the "learning disabilities lifestyle" was dominating his life, and making him miserable, and asking about his willingness to challenge this lifestyle, they prescribed a number of tasks. One of these involved an observation that the boy seemed particularly to lose his ability to concentrate and follow-through with his work in the period immediately prior to breaks. He was told that a "special assignment" would be prescribed just before recess, and this assignment would be designed to "test" his readiness to challenge the disabilities. Moreover, various "stimuli" had been identified as "common distractors" that interfered with his concentration in the classroom. During his work on his "special assignment", his teacher was to introduce these "distractors", sometimes in an exaggerated way, at irregular and unpredictable intervals. The boy was able to complete his assignment, ignoring the imposed distractions. This success was used to help him identify the special skills he had used, and a similar task was used at home, regarding his homework. (from Stewart & Nodrick, 1990)

A number of techniques were used with this boy, including "externalising the problem" (the "learning disabilities lifestyle" was dominating his life, and making him miserable — see White, 1989), a challenge in an "experimental" situation (the assignment was described as being simply to test his readiness, not treat his problem), and the deliberate exaggeration of seemingly random events (the distractions). The task may also have altered the teacher's usual pattern of response to the boy's lack of concentration. What the task did *not* involve was further assessment or repeated attempts at remedial education, which had been shown not to work.

I saw a 7-year-old girl, Julia, who was unable to sleep in her own bed, and unable to go into any room in the house without her parents, and there were frequent episodes of terror, screaming and subsequent argument. The problem seemed to have stemmed from a traumatic experience when the family home had been burgled, and Julia had been the one to discover the evidence of the burglary.

I talked with Julia for some time about her bedroom, and the things she enjoyed about it. She described her pink bedroom, her teddy bear, and her enjoyment of bedtime stories. We discussed various books that she enjoyed reading and I discovered that her favourite was the 'Mr Men' series. For no particular reason, and without any thought of a clever intervention, I asked Julia if she had read 'Mr Scarey'. She took delight in informing me that there was not a 'Mr Scarey' in the series (I did not confess to her that, when I had asked the question, I could not remember whether or not such a title existed!).

I began to ask Julia what she thought might be in the story of 'Mr. Scarey' if it did exist and, as she engaged in this discussion enthusiastically, it struck me that this might be a way to harness Julia's enthusiasm and imagination to get her doing something practical that might be helpful. Being an expert on 'Mr. Men' books, Julia told me that the story would include Mr. Scarey and one other person (The Mr Men books always involve the main character and a second character who acts as something of a 'foil' and usually finishes in the 'one-up' position). I wondered if the other person would be a little girl, and Julia suggested that it would be a girl of about her age. She decided to call her 'Peta'.

I speculated that Peta might be scared by Mr. Scarey, because she might not realise that he really wasn't as scarey as he pretended. Julia thought this might be the case, and was pleased when I suggested that perhaps she could start to write the story of Peta and Mr. Scarey.

Two weeks later, the family returned and Julia appeared a little more animated than before. She insisted on showing me her story immediately. Mum had purchased a new exercise book for Julia and had helped her cover it in bright paper, and Julia had written four pages of the story of 'Mr. Scarey'.

We talked about her beautiful artwork and the story she had written. I was especially interested in page four, which said that Peta was going to scare Mr. Scarey and say 'Boo' to him. Peta told me that the story was not finished, and I wondered how it would end. I wondered if she thought Mr. Scarey would get bigger and bigger and Peta get smaller and smaller, or if maybe Peta would get bigger and bigger and Mr. Scarey get smaller and smaller. She said she thought Peta would get bigger. (from Durrant, 1990)

The referral of this girl had suggested that I help her "come to terms with" her fears. I did not set out to do that — although perhaps that is what happened. Certainly, I did not explore the nature of the fears or the event that seemed to have triggered them in any detail. Once the girl in the story stopped being scared, so did my client.

What each of these examples has in common is more in terms of what did *not* happen in the counselling or intervention than what did happen. They also do not necessarily seem commonsense.

There are many ideas about what is "necessary" for children, adolescents and adults to do in order that they resolve their emotional, behavioural or educational problems. When these ideas are helpful, then we should make the most of them. My experience is that school counsellors often find that *either* they do not have the time or resources to do justice to some ideas about what should happen in therapy *or* they find themselves stuck in situations where what "should" work does not seem to.

This book seeks to offer some ways of thinking about, and intervening in, the kinds of problems that arise in schools — ways that might work. I begin with some thoughts about the role of theory and assumptions in counselling and therapy, since the ideas rest on very different principles from those most of us were taught in psychology lectures. Building on the discussion of theory, the book seeks to present practical strategies for dealing with problems the kinds of problems that school psychologists face, and I have tried to illustrate the various ideas with examples from my own work and from the work of others.

The strategies aim to be *practical* and *simple*— however, that does not always mean they will be *easy*. The competing demands from the various parts of the school system will often challenge our beliefs in our own competence! Nonetheless, the book reflects ideas I have presented in numerous workshops, and which people have said they found helpful. The book also reflects the ways in which my ideas have been challenged and changed by the comments of the teachers, counsellors and parents with whom I have talked.

For some, the ideas (coming, as they do, from the field of the "brief therapies") will be familiar. For others, the principles will be new, perhaps challenging and may seem to contradict ideas on which counselling has traditionally been based.

To paraphrase two of the essential (and essentially pragmatic) principles which underpin the brief therapy approaches —

- If what you are doing with students and teachers is working, then keep doing it.

- If there are times when it is not working, then perhaps this book will help you consider something different.

— Michael Durrant
Epping, NSW
March 1993

ACKNOWLEDGEMENTS

This book owes much to the teachers and counsellors who have shared ideas with me over the last few years.

Kate Kowalski was my partner in my therapy practice for a couple of years. Kate and I conducted a number of workshops for School Counsellors and Kate has been an integral part of the development of my ideas. When I refer to "we" or "our" in this manuscript, I am referring to work that Kate and I have done together. She is now back in the United States, however Kate continues to be important to me in helping me clarify what it is that I think I do.

Susan Barrows Munro from W W Norton & Company has allowed me to reproduce brief quotations from various books published by Norton, for which I am grateful, and Ron Kral not only has taught me much about working with teachers but also has given his permission for me to reproduce extracts from various of his publications.

Brian Cade, my valued colleague, read various versions of the manuscript, allowed me to steal a few ideas, and told me which bits did not make sense. Jane Durrant and Marjory Cade put the book together.

I HOW DO WE THINK about SCHOOL PROBLEMS?

In many ways, the demands of our therapeutic contact with students and colleagues is to "get on with it" — the pressures of dealing with classroom and school difficulties day-to-day are immediate and strong, and there often is little time to reflect on why we do the things we do. To most of us, the idea of "theory" is interesting on occasions, when we have the time to engage in reflective discussion, but the rest of the time we have a job to do and we have ways of doing it that are familiar.

Of course, theory has a place, since (formally or otherwise) we will try to make sense of the behaviour of the students with whom we have contact. The way we try to deal with a problem situation will flow from the way we make sense of it. Often, there is pressure on us (as psychologists) to come up with an explanation of why a student is doing this or that. Unfortunately, there is no way of really knowing, absolutely and for sure, *why* a person does a particular thing or what some behaviour means. Lots of people will assert, very, very definitely, that the reason for some behaviour is such-and-such — the problem is that other people will assert, equally definitely, that the reason is something else! In fact, we don't know (and my experience is that children and adults often genuinely don't know why they do things either) — all we do is make sensible guesses; guesses that help us with our task.

A theory is a kind of "map" that helps us make consistent guesses, and being consistent is important. No "model" of therapy is "true", in that the concepts (such as "family system", "boundaries", "rules", "self-esteem", and so on) do not actually exist as entities within our clients. Rather, a model is a map, or metaphor, which we therapists place on what we see to allow us to make some sense of it. Ultimately, a model may be more or less helpful for us as therapists, but not more or less true or accurate. Essentially, the value of a map is that it helps us determine how to get from 'A' to 'B'. Most of our clients simply want to get to 'B' (the solution). Similarly, teachers, principals and parents simply want us to help get the student to 'B'. They may have ideas about what needs to happen, however their major concern is usually that the problem be solved, so life can proceed.

I find the idea of a "theory" or "model" of therapy as a **map** a helpful one. If I have to travel from Sydney to Melbourne, I have a choice of maps to help me get there. My "BP Road Atlas" shows the names and numbers of the highways and cities, and the BP service stations along the way. My old geographical map shows none of these, but shows the rivers, the lakes, the mountains, and so on. Both maps help me figure out how to get there, and neither is more "true" than the other — they just choose to focus on different aspects. However, which map I use will have a significant impact on the way the journey progresses. If I use the Road Atlas, I will judge my progress by noticing the cities and the BP stations (and may not even notice the lakes and rivers). If I use the geographical map, I will judge my progress by noticing landforms I pass (and may not even notice the BP stations). That is, the map we use will not only determine how we plan the journey, but will also dictate what we notice along the way. Also, whatever map we use, it is quite possible to concentrate so closely on the map that we run off the road! I have seen many therapists (including myself) do this! A number of people have considered models of therapy as maps, including de Shazer (1988) and Blymyer & Smith (1992). (As I will elaborate later, de Shazer suggests that, rather than thinking about the best "route" to get where we are going with clients, the more important question is "How will we know when we get there?")

Counselling or behaviour intervention in schools is ultimately pragmatic — everyone, from the Principal down, just wants things to change and usually does not care too much how we do it. On the other hand, everyone has some idea about *why* the behaviour is happening and *what* needs to happen. My view is that we should test our "theories" on similarly pragmatic lines

— does our way of making sense of a situation help us work towards a solution? For example, it may or may not be true that a student's consistent poor behaviour is related to the fact that he or she has an alcoholic parent. However, there is very little that we can do to change that situation. Thus, an explanation in terms of parental alcoholism (or various other "fixed" characteristics) is likely to immobilise us. It is common for people to explain a student's behaviour in terms of family events or characteristics ("Dad just lost his job", "Mum is depressed", "he is a middle child", and so on) or in terms of personality or psychological 'traits' ("He is impulsive", "She is conduct disordered", "He is just like that", and so on). My concern is *not* with whether or not these explanations are "true" — but with whether they allow the school counsellor and teachers some idea about how to deal with the problem.

In seeking to work with students and teachers, we need theoretical concepts that give us a way forward. I have found a particular set of ideas helpful in my work, and try to use them fairly consistently in all aspects of my work in therapy. The ideas come from a particular approach to brief therapy, however I see them as a way of thinking about people and behaviour rather than just a way of doing therapy.

IDEAS OF "REALITY"

The family therapy field has been characterised by discussions about "epistemology" (the theory of knowledge — or how we know what we think and what we think we think). Lately, the debate has centred around those who adopt a "constructivist" perspective and those who do not.

Constructivism is the view that "reality", or what we "know" about the world and our experience of it, is a product of our own mental processes rather than representing something that actually exists. That is, a constructivist perspective rests on the notion that all we really know about the world is our experience of it and the way we make sense of it. We are all engaged in a constant process of making sense of what we experience. Different things mean different things to different people. Some people regard things as problems that others find normal and acceptable. For Bateson, context was a central idea. Nothing makes sense outside its context, since the same event may mean different things if made sense of differently. The constructivist position suggests that it is the way things are made sense of that is the important element for therapy.

Counselling or therapy is concerned with people's perceptions of, or beliefs about, themselves, their behaviour and the world — for it is these beliefs or perceptions that determine behaviour. Hence, any attempt to change behaviour necessarily involves changing meaning. Moreover, constructivism suggests that "reality" has something to do with the process of observation. That is, as therapists, we are engaged in a process of making sense of what we see with our clients and the conclusions to which we come cannot be separated from the process of our observing and interpreting. Therapies which adopt this perspective are concerned more with the experience of our clients, and how they make sense of that experience, than with so-called objective meanings, diagnoses or classifications.

From this perspective, any analysis of problem situations within schools will include an examination of how the people concerned make sense of the particular behaviour or situation. For example, in looking at persistent difficulty a teacher has with a particular child, we will wish to consider the way the TEACHER makes sense of the behaviour as well as how the student does. How the teacher makes sense of it will determine the teacher's response. Over time, teacher and student may well become stuck in a repetitive pattern. Often, helping the teacher make sense of the behaviour differently will lead to a different response which, since it breaks the pattern, will lead to different behaviour on the part of the student.

Many parents (and teachers) have employed techniques of trying to turn (mis)behaviour into a game. Kral (1989a) gives the example of a boy who precipitated vehement fights about going to bed and the results of a parent saying "you look like a fast little boy, how quickly can you make it up to bed? I'll time you". Epston (1984) recounts a story of a boy who stole money but refused to admit that he had done so. His father said something like, "You know, I can't understand it, but I seem to have lost fifty cents. Can you help me find it?". The ritual that ensued involved father and son each looking in a different room, coming back and admitting that they had not found the money, searching different rooms, not finding the money, and so on ... until, finally, the boy went to search his own room while Father searched his. When the boy returned, having "found" the money, his father was appropriately grateful. The father repeated this procedure on each of the next few days (even though money had not been stolen) and, miraculously, the boy always found the allegedly missing money in his room. Father was so grateful that he allowed his son to keep the money, and the son stopped stealing.

This technique is familiar to many. Making the situation into a game not only changes the meaning of the situation, it also changes the pattern of adult-child interaction that has developed around the problem. Of course, for the adult to respond differently required that they think differently about the situation. It is unclear to what extent the change led to a change in the characteristic reaction of the adult, or to a change in the meaning for the child. It also probably doesn't matter.

Another example from a school setting:

A teacher sought advice on how to deal with a particularly difficult student. He had come to the school from a special, child psychiatry unit, and had been preceded by what seemed like a truck-load of assessment information. The staff had been warned that this boy had extreme temper outbursts when he experienced frustration. The staff of the psychiatric unit, eager to help the transition to school succeed, had instituted a procedure whereby the school staff would phone the unit if the boy had an extreme tantrum, and a special nurse would come immediately to the school to help manage the situation.

The teachers were feeling fearful of the boy and his tantrums, and were not sure they could run the risk of waiting for the nurse to arrive.

The consultation group suggested that, perhaps, we had been thinking about this boy in the wrong way. It was easy to see him as someone with extreme psychiatric problems. Perhaps that was not what was important. Perhaps we needed to recognise that he was a boy who had experienced numerous changes in his life, education and accommodation — that he was probably feeling extremely insecure and confused.

We speculated on what difference it might make to think about him in this way. Someone suggested that it would mean that it was important that teachers help him feel "secure" by dealing with his behaviour firmly and clearly, so he could "know where he stood".

As long as the staff thought of him as "special" (a boy with a psychiatric condition), they felt immobilised. The plan that a psychiatric nurse would come to "rescue" them — whilst well-meaning — simply helped fuel their sense of impotence. We can safely assume that the boy would sense the staff's feelings of helplessness and would respond to that. Boy and staff had become stuck in a pattern of mutual expectation and response which was self-defeating.

The different way of thinking about the boy gave the staff "permission" to attempt to manage his behaviour. It would still not be easy — however they were more likely to feel that they were doing something, and he was more likely to respond to their increased confidence.

This is not to say that the teachers' responses were the "cause" of the problem — far from it. However, it suggests that solutions do not necessarily relate to causes, and that changing one part of an interaction often changes the other parts. Change may involve helping people THINK differently (which will usually lead to their behaving differently), or it may more directly involve helping people to ACT differently (which will usually lead to their developing a different view of the situation).

This is a simple idea — that the solutions to problems are not necessarily related to the apparent causes of problems — however it has profound implications. If intervention MUST address causes, our task becomes daunting, particularly when there seems little we can do about the apparent cause (except, perhaps, refer the case to someone else, which is never very satisfying). If, on the other hand, we can find a way to help students and teachers do something different — something which relieves the situation — WITHOUT always having to find and deal with the cause, the idea might be liberating.

Murphy comments on the implications of constructivism for the school situation:

> For example, students and others may hold very different views as to whether or not a problem even exists, as well as varying ideas about its cause or solution. The constructivist notion says that we act on a particular meaning (e.g., "disinterested, apathetic student") as if it were the only truth about the problem, instead of merely one of several plausible meanings for the same events or behaviours (e.g., "quiet, respectful observer").
>
> In this approach, the validity of a specific meaning or interpretation is based strictly on a pragmatic clinical criterion — its utility in promoting a different response to the problem on the part of the student or concerned others. Since meanings are pragmatically selected based on the idiosyncratic aspects of the problem and people involved, the usefulness of specific interpretations (e.g., irrational thoughts, family dysfunction, hyperactivity) will vary from case to case.
>
> Constructivism inherently acknowledges the complexity of human behaviour, its origins, and interpretation. Adoption of this perspective allows practitioners optimal flexibility in interpreting behaviour in clinically useful ways, without compromising their genuineness or sincerity.
>
> — (Murphy, 1992, p. 62)

Whilst the discussion of constructivism and "reality" becomes somewhat esoteric at times, it does have practical relevance to counselling in schools.

As suggested above, it allows us to focus on "what works" rather than becoming embroiled in what is "true". Moreover, it is relevant when we consider "motivation" of students towards counselling, since a student may not be motivated to "work on" a particular problem but may be motivated if the problem is described or understood differently. This will be elaborated later.

Similarly, when dealing with behaviour and emotion, a focus on what this behaviour means to the particular people involved, rather than in rela tion to some more-or-less objective criteria, may have different implications for activities such as assessment.

Even when we are dealing with more (apparently) objective problems, such as educational problems, this perspective may make a difference. If a student is responding to remedial input, then this should continue. However, if remedial input appears to be making little difference, and teachers seem to be working harder and harder to solve the problem, while the student appears to be standing still, then a different approach is warranted. In this situation, we might consider that — whatever disabilities, deficits or problems might be leading to the learning problem — the way it is being addressed has perhaps become part of the problem, and a change in the way things are dealt with might lead to people thinking differently about it.

Molnar and Lindquist (1989) suggest, "when you want something to change, you must change something". If we are preoccupied with the "real" meaning, or cause, of a problem, we may find it hard to identify what must be changed. However, if we accept that the meaning of the problem, at the moment, for the people involved, is what matters, we might find the opportunity to change *something*, and so alter the whole interactional meaning.

Molnar and Lindquist focus on meaning within the interactional context and use the term "the ecosystemic approach".

> Regarding schools and classrooms as ecosystems means that the behaviour of everyone in the classroom or school in which the problem occurs influences and is influenced by that problem behaviour. From this perspective a change in the perception or behaviour of anyone associated with the problem has the potential to influence the problem behaviour. We believe this is a very hopeful point of view because it says that everyone in a problem situation has the capacity to influence it positively.   — (Molnar & Lindquist, 1989, p. xiv)

Again, a focus on meaning and behaviour allows the possibility of bringing about change by making a small change somewhere, whether or not we have been able to discover the "true" cause. It allows us to work towards a solution, confident that, if we can get one part of the problem interaction to be different, it will have an effect on everyone else involved.

By the time a "problem" comes to the attention of a counsellor, it will have attracted a variety of explanations and ideas about what needs to happen to solve it.

Often, these explanations will be in terms of traumatic incidents, family dysfunction, or personality characteristics of the student or parents.

These may, or may not, be "true". By and large, however, these explanations will not suggest a way that the counsellor may help solve the problem.

Explanations such as "his parents separated" leave counsellors and teachers immobilised — it is difficult to reverse a parental separation within the school situation — thus school personnel are left with no options.

A theory or "map" that provides no options is not very helpful.

We need a map for counselling that "works" — whether or not it seems to focus on the underlying issues — it needs to provide a way for counsellors to be able to be effective and useful.

COMMON ASSUMPTIONS

ABOUT SCHOOL PROBLEMS

- school problems are someone's fault ... the child's, the parents', the teacher's, etc.;

- school problems are the result of some personal (psychological) or family deficiencies;

- problem behaviour in the school includes only the student's behaviour, which might be modified (regardless of other people's behaviour or responses);

- if behaviour modification is insufficient, the psychological deficiencies need to be understood and 'worked through' in order to avoid further emotional problems or further difficulties at school;

- problems which manifest themselves in difficult school behaviour are likely to result in future maladjustments;

- once we understand the reason/cause of the difficulty we will then know how to 'fix' it.

(Adapted from a similar table first compiled by Kate Kowalski)

MY ASSUMPTIONS

ABOUT SCHOOL PROBLEMS

- school problems are best viewed in terms of interactional patterns which are inadvertently maintained in the hope of resolving the original difficulty;

- Whatever may have 'caused' it, a school problem often persists because the student, and/or the teachers, and/or the parents continue to respond to it in a way that inadvertently helps it continue;

- school problems do not necessarily reflect any type of individual, school or family deficiency;

- it is most useful to look at developing a solution to the problem(s), rather than understanding the 'cause', particularly since school personnel often cannot do anything about the apparent cause;

- school problems, like other difficulties, have a tendency to escalate into 'vicious cycles' which serve to reinforce a 'problem-focused' view of the student and/or teacher involved;

- such 'cycles' tend to overshadow information about any aspects of the student involved which challenge the problem-focused description;

- a change in the "problem" behaviour can lead to far-reaching changes which have positive effects on many aspects of future behaviour and functioning.

THE MAIN ASSUMPTIONS OF A BRIEF, INTERACTIONAL APPROACH

1. People are engaged in a constant process of making sense of their experience.

This is a process of forming presuppositions about interaction and behaviour (what Kelly called "personal constructs"), since we all need presuppositions about the world to help us manage from day to day. Behaviour is consistent with the way self, others and situations are experienced and made sense of. Beliefs about self and others keep people from noticing information about themselves, others, or relationships that would allow them to notice differences and move forward.

2. People experience problems as problems and generally want things to be better.

Any behaviour may have a variety of "meanings", some positive and some negative, and problem behaviour might "make sense" — that is, "problem behaviour" is based on a particular view of reality which can be understood, respected and co-operated with. It is unhelpful to think in terms of resistance, addiction, disorder or denial — people's differing "motivation" fits with their view of the situation and the possibility of change.

3. Problems do not indicate pathology.

Problems occur in the context of human interaction and, usually, problems "just happen". Problem patterns include both behaviour and perceptions. Both behaving differently and thinking differently are part of the process of change. It is more helpful to consider, "what gets in the way of the client(s) finding or noticing solutions?" than, "what caused this problem?"

4. People have tried to solve their problems

... but the attempts have not worked. These attempted solutions (derived

Whether we acknowledge it or not, our work with students and colleagues is based on a set of assumptions about people, problems, behaviour and change. That is, because we cannot "know" why things happen, we have a set of guiding principles and "assume" things that fit with these.

from the client's construction of the problem) frequently lead people to focus more on the problem, and feeling stuck, than on alternate solutions.

5. People have within them a wealth of resources.

These resources are both known and unknown to them. One of the main effects of problems, and peoples' experience of them, is to blind people from noticing their strengths and capabilities, or the solution-oriented behaviour that already exists. They develop a "problem-dominated" view of self and interaction. People tend to notice and place greater emphasis on "facts" which support this view of themselves, others, relationships, and situations.

6. The problem is the problem

The person is not the problem. Notions of pathology, dysfunction, purposiveness, functionality or diagnostic labels suggest that problems are part of people, which leaves them unable to experience themselves as having any personal agency in finding the solution.

7. Change is constant

Change is inevitable. The snowball effect ... small change can lead to bigger change. The best changes are those identified by the client rather than the therapist, and these can be seen as part of a process of small steps.

... continued

(This list of assumptions is adapted from a handout originally prepared by Kate Kowalski and myself.)

8. Every problem-dominated pattern includes examples of EXCEPTIONS

These exceptions (times when the problem is *not* happening, or something different is happening) serve as hints towards solution. Typically not seen as significant by the clients, they can be given meaning through the process of questioning about them. Focusing on these small "chinks" in the client's behaviour or self-perception be as a foundation on which she/he can build a new view of herself as competent and in-control.

9. The problem can be "framed" differently — and more helpfully

New and beneficial meanings can be constructed for at least some aspect of the client's complaint ... the problem can be redefined in a way that helpe identify existing solution-behaviour and/or opens the possibility of new solution-oriented behaviour. Solution ideas (interventions) work best when they fit with the clients' world view, language, and experience.

10. "If it works, don't fix it."

Encourage clients to do more of it. "If it's not working, do something different". These ideas are important not only for clients but also for therapists.

11. You don't need to know what the problem is.

Effective therapy can be done even when the therapist cannot describe exactly what the problem is, or when clients don't agree on the definition of the problem. It is more important to know what will be different when the problem is solved.

2   CHANGING BEHAVIOUR and MEANING

The "brief therapy" field has much to offer counsellors who want a commonsense approach that seeks to change behaviour and meanings, without becoming embroiled in the archaeology of causes. Brief therapy tends to be pragmatic (but is not just concerned with symptom-removal) and is concerned with simplicity as much as possible. This seems quite different from those approaches which seem to value complexity in language and classification.

ERICKSON'S APPROACH

Many of the approaches that are now called "brief therapy" or "family therapy" have been influenced by the work of Milton Erickson.

Psychiatrist and hypnotherapist, Milton Erickson was dyslexic, tone deaf and colour-blind. He suffered polio at 17 and again at 51. His first attack left him almost totally paralysed, however he demonstrated a determination to rehabilitate himself. In the process of doing so, he developed extraordinary powers of observation (he taught himself to walk again by observing minutely the processes by which his infant sister mastered walking, and then using these observations to visualize himself moving certain muscles, etc. and to practice particular movements). He developed a belief that limitations were somehow a mental construct and that normally overlooked resources could be tapped in overcoming the power of disability.

Erickson seems to have developed a view of life as a continuing experiment in which the most seemingly insurmountable obstacle became a challenge to his resourcefulness, creativity and iron will. ... It was as if the young Erickson's illness ... gave him a glimpse into the superstructure of subjective reality. ... He discovered that most of the "rules" of life prescribing human limitations were arbitrary beliefs, not facts. As he put it, many years later "Human beings, being human, tend to react in patterns and we are governed by patterns of behaviour ... You don't realize how very rigidly patterned all of us are."

What emerges again and again in reading accounts of Erickson's work was his ability to tune into the unique subjective world of the particular person or persons he was treating ... with his great acuity, he was able to discern the foundations of the distinctive pattern of reality underlying a person's behaviour.

Erickson was notoriously leery of theoretical generalizations. He continuously reminded his students that a categorical approach to the study of people, or any subject, denies the cardinal reality of individual differences and discourages the use of one of the therapist's most essential tools — his powers of observation. (Simon, 1983)

Erickson's work, both in hypnosis and in his use of "hypnotic" principles about communication, language and change in non-hypnotic situations, was characterised by a profound respect for the *experience* of the people with whom he worked. Having sought to understand, and validate, his clients' experience (rather than the presuppositions of other professionals), he used therapeutic interventions that introduced a different perspective or different behaviour. Whilst Erickson's interventions sometimes appeared "tricky" — because they did not fit prevailing ideas about what kinds of solutions were necessary — they always reflected a profound respect for the particular (and often idiosyncratic) way in which the client made sense of him or herself.

Fundamental to Erickson's work was the notion of *utilization* — the notion that it is not useful to engage in "combat" with clients whose ideas do not seem to fit with the therapist's ideas, rather we must find ways to use whatever it is that the client brings. "Utilizing whatever the client does that is somehow 'right,' 'useful'. 'effective,' 'good' or 'fun', for the purposes of developing a solution" (de Shazer, 1988, p.140).

> One of Erickson's better-known (and more bizarre) cases — which has nothing to do with the school situation — involved what he termed "the indirect hypnotic treatment of a bedwetting couple". The couple, both very inhibited and strongly religious, both had a bedwetting problem but neither was aware of the other's problem. After their wedding night, they awoke to find a wet bed. The man lay there, feeling embarrassed, and thinking "isn't she wonderful, she's not saying anything about it." The woman lay there, feeling embarrassed, and thinking "isn't he wonderful, he's not saying anything about it." It was some time before they realised that they *both* had the same problem.
>
> Erickson asked them to agree that they would do whatever he suggested to solve the problem. He instructed them both to kneel on the bed each night, before going to sleep, and deliberately urinate on the bed. He added that they were to drink lots of fluids in the few hours before bed. Further, they were not to discuss the task.
>
> The couple reported that they had a dry bed after two weeks. Further, although their embarrassment had inhibited sex after their wedding night, they later brought their baby to visit Erickson. (reported by O'Hanlon & Hexum, 1990 and Rossi, 1980)

This positive outcome is open to a number of explanations (and, by and large, the various accounts of Erickson's work suggest that he was not overly interested in speculating about why something had worked.). Erickson gained the couple's trust; he had them do something different from their usual pattern of trying to stop wetting the bed; he prescribed (or utilized) the problem, but in a different way; and he gave them something of an "ordeal".

By and large, Erickson understood problems in terms of "habit", bound within a particular context — he did not focus on ideas about the "function" or "secondary gain" of a problem, but had an emphasis on people's positive intent and an emphasis on change, no matter how small.

Erickson's influence is evident in a variety of the family therapy approaches, such as the MRI Brief Therapy approach, the Solution-Focused Brief Therapy approach and Haley's strategic approach, as well as in Michael White's ideas. Many of the "family therapy" models have acknowledged the influence of Gregory Bateson. Erickson's contribution has sometimes been less well acknowledged, however he was an important part of the development of brief, interactional approaches.

MRI BRIEF THERAPY APPROACH

The Brief Therapy project at the Mental Research Institute in Palo Alto (California) laid down many of the essential ideas that underpin brief and commonsense approaches (Weakland et al, 1974). Their work was based upon many of Milton Erickson's ideas, as well as the ideas of Gregory Bateson (the MRI Brief Therapy Project "grew" out of the group who worked with Bateson on his research project into the interactional basis of schizophrenia, a project which used Erickson as a clinical consultant).

In a time where therapy was always long-term, and was founded on "traditional" psychiatric ideas about underlying causes and lengthy, insight-oriented exploration, the MRI Brief Therapy Project sought to see what would happen if they limited therapy to 10 sessions. This entailed the development of an approach that focused on the resolution of problems, and on clients developing a successful life and future, rather than seeking to deal with every experience, thought or feeling that might be assumed to have some bearing on the development of the problem.

> We are frankly symptom-oriented, in a broad sense. Patients or their family members come with certain complaints and accepting them for treatment involves a responsibility for relieving these complaints. Also, since deviant symptomatic behaviour and its accompanying vicious cycles of reaction and counter-reaction can themselves be so disruptive of system

functioning, we believe that one should not hasten to seek other and deeper roots of pathology. The presenting problem offers, in one package, what the patient is ready to work on, a concentrated manifestation of whatever is wrong, and a concrete index of any progress made. (Weakland et al, 1974, p 147).

Most of the developments within the fields of brief and family therapy build, to a greater or lesser extent, on the principles and strategies of the MRI group. Fundamental to their approach are ideas such as:

Problems just happen

Problems arise from ordinary (or extraordinary) difficulties, made sense of in a particular way. Murphy (1992, p. 62) comments,

> A problem process develops when ordinary difficulties in a student's life, such as peer conflict or academic problems, are mishandled by the student or others. The difficulty then becomes viewed as a problem, and the well-intentioned efforts to resolve it on the part of the student or others actually make it worse. ... Intervention is directed toward interrupting ineffective solution attempts in order to allow for more productive responses to the problem.

For example, frustration when faced with teasing is a normal situation — it may become a problem when the student makes sense of it in terms of his or her own failure, becomes less confident, and so becomes more likely to get upset, etc.

Problems persist because of problem-maintaining interaction

No matter what the "cause" might be, problems continue because the client and/or other people with whom the client interacts behave in ways that inadvertently maintain them. It is usually peoples' *attempted solutions*

— the things they do that try to deal with the problem, in their view — that help maintain it.

For example, a student's forgetfulness and lack of concentration may or may not be due to her preoccupation with her parents' looming marriage break-up. However, as a teacher becomes more and more concerned about the problem, he or she might respond to the student by encouraging, pushing and reminding even more (in many ways, a completely "reasonable" response). The student, whilst perhaps getting irritated by the teacher's constant reminders, does not experience herself as remembering or achieving things herself. Thus she gets caught in an escalating cycle whereby she thinks of herself as unable to do her work and behaves in accordance with this view.

New behaviour can interrupt problem-maintaining patterns

Behaviour on the part of anyone involved in the interaction that is NOT part of the usual pattern may interrupt the problem-maintaining pattern and so free the system to respond differently. The new behaviour does not necessarily have to "make sense".

For example, if strenuous efforts to extinguish certain behaviour have inadvertently helped maintain it, a new response that appears to encourage the behaviour may (paradoxically) interrupt the usual pattern and lead to new behaviour.

New meanings can interrupt problem-maintaining patterns

REFRAMING is defined as "... to change the conceptual and/or emotional setting or viewpoint in relation to which a situation is experienced and to place it in another frame which fits the 'facts' of the same concrete situation equally well or even better, and thereby changes its entire meaning." (Watzlawick, Weakland, and Fisch, 1974, p.95) A different meaning or frame offers people an opportunity to make sense of their experience differently and so to have the option of behaving and feeling differently.

Molnar & Lindquist (1989) give an example of a group of boys who spent much of each lesson conducting loud conversations across the classroom. The teacher interpreted this as "defiant and disruptive behaviour" and responded accordingly — however her attempts at control were unsuccessful, and she and the students became caught in an escalating pattern. When the teacher was able to reframe the behaviour as "friendships are important and these students need to keep in contact in order to nurture their friendship", she saw the situation less in terms of a power struggle. So, she encouraged the students to spend time "catching up with each other", and specified a time at the beginning of each lesson when they were encouraged to talk together. As she then responded differently, the students gradually ceased their disruption.

SOLUTION FOCUSED BRIEF THERAPY

de Shazer and his colleagues at the Brief Family Therapy Center, Milwaukee, developed their approach, based on Erickson's ideas about people's resources and sharing many ideas with the MRI approach. Their work led them away from a problem focus to solution construction with clients when they recognised that what clients found helpful ("solutions") often appeared to have no direct relationship to the problems presented, but in some way "fitted" with the clients' experience (de Shazer, 1985). As a result, the emphasis of treatment shifted from trying to understand the problem and how to help clients solve it, to asking clients questions and prescribing tasks to help them focus on their own perception of needs, goals and their own existing and potential resources for solutions (Lipchik & de Shazer, 1986; Molnar & de Shazer, 1987). Problems are what get people stuck, and a focus on these may lead to more stuckness. Solutions are the changes people strive for, and a focus on these allows us to be more forward looking.

Whilst some complain that it is "simplistic", the solution-focused approach has been used successfully with a range of client populations and problems — including longterm alcohol problems (Berg & Miller, 1992; Blymyer & Smith, 1992), marital difficulties (Hudson & O'Hanlon, 1992; de Shazer, 1991); sexual abuse (Dolan, 1991; Durrant & Kowalski, 1990);

depression (Durrant & Kowalski, 1993); residential treatment of adolescents (Durrant, 1993); psychiatric disorders (de Shazer, 1991, chap 12); and so on — and Molnar & Lindquist (1989) and Kral (1988, 1989a and b) have applied the approach specifically to the school situation.

Exceptions

Asking clients about times when the problem wasn't a problem (or was less so) is often more helpful than asking about the times it was a problem. In many ways, it is easier to "build on" what is already going right than to "fix" what is going wrong.

> Problems are seen to maintain themselves simply because they maintain themselves and because clients depict problems as always happening. Therefore, times when the complaint is absent are dismissed as trivial by the client or even remain completely unseen, hidden from the client's view. Nothing is actually hidden, but although these exceptions are open to view, they are not seen by the client as differences that make a difference. For the client, the problem is seen as primary (and the exceptions, if seen at all, are seen as secondary), while for therapists the exceptions are seen as primary; interventions are meant to help clients make a similar inversion, which will lead to the development of a solution. (de Shazer, 1991, p. 58)

> For example, a student who is constantly failing to finish work and so becomes disruptive may not respond to strategies designed to change this behaviour. The student may develop a view of "I can't do it", or "I don't care", and further efforts at changing the behaviour simply seem to confirm this. However, a focus on those (perhaps rare and perhaps small) examples of times that the student managed to finish some work may give teacher and/or student a different perspective. It may be that a focus on these small successes helps the teacher form a different view and so respond differently, or it may be that a discussion of such exceptions will lead to the student being able to try to do more of "what is already working".

Utilization

The Solution-Focused Model's emphasis on strength and solutions is a direct reliance on Erickson's idea of *utilization*. When Erickson "taught" himself to walk again, and concluded that limitations were only mental constructs, this was NOT a blind faith in human goodness or resources. Rather, it was as if the young Erickson said, "Well, I obviously learned to walk once before, so I must have whatever it takes to be able to do it". That is, Erickson's belief was that people have the learning and skills, in their past experiences, to be able to deal with most challenges. His approach was to utilize these past learnings that otherwise went unrecognised.

Further, he came to believe that we could utilize *whatever* a client brought to therapy — even if it seemed like resistance or lack of motivation.

> We view [therapy] as a process whereby we help people utilize their own mental associations, memories and life potentials to achieve their own therapeutic goals. [Therapy] can facilitate the utilization of abilities and potentials that already exist within a person but that remain unused or underdeveloped ... the [therapist] ... explores a patient's individuality to ascertain what life learnings, experiences, and mental skills are available to deal with the problem. (Erickson & Rossi, 1979, p.1)

The belief that we can utilize *whatever* it is that clients (students, teachers, or parents) bring allows us to believe that currently, or previously, successful behaviour (exceptions) can be harnessed in the process of change. Moreover, it is this belief that allows us to dispense with concepts such as "resistance". A focus on utilization allows the solution-focused therapist to find *something* to use — something that can be seen as the client's "cooperation".

> Each family (individual or couple) shows a unique way of attempting to cooperate ... If a therapist *chooses* to see the client's behavior as resistance, then their attempts to cooperate cannot be seen, since one view precludes the other; if a thera

pist is looking for cooperative behavior, then he will be unable
to see resistance. (de Shazer, 1985, pp. 72–73)

One tangible outworking of this principle is in the setting of a therapeutic
agenda with students who do not think they have a problem. As is explained
later, we can utilise their attitude (which might otherwise be seen as "denial"
or "resistance") by establishing the goal of counselling as "proving to teachers that you do not have a problem".

Future focus

The ability to imagine the future solution state (what things will be like
when the problem is solved) is a powerful resource for people. There are a
variety of "future focused" questions which ask clients to describe, in detail,
the future solution and then seek to help them achieve this. The very fact of
being able to describe the solution seems to make it more achievable.

> We all live in our past, our present and our future ... [and]
> our perception of all of these is a highly selective one. The
> future exists in our anticipation of how it will be. Traditionally,
> therapies have concerned themselves with the past and with the
> present, with attempting to effect changes in them through a
> process of re-examination .What is new and exciting in the
> field is that it appears that the future is also open for re-
> examination even though it has not yet happened. (Cade &
> O'Hanlon, 1993, p 109)

> A positive view of the future invites hope, and hope in its
> turn helps to cope with current hardships, to recognize signs
> indicating the possibility of change, to view the past as an
> ordeal rather than a misery, and to provide the inspiration for
> generating solutions (Furman & Ahola, 1992, p. 91)

> For example, a Year 3 boy had ongoing problems with day-
> dreaming, silliness in class and becoming extremely upset when
> things did not go right. An exploration of the problem (its history,
> incidence, etc.) seemed to lead to everyone becoming more and more

despondent and less hopeful about the possibility of change. Within this context, any suggestions to the boy, his mother, or the teacher were either met with "that probably wouldn't work", or with a resigned agreement to try the suggestion, which ultimately failed. After we discussed at some length the fact that he felt "silly" and childish when he was in trouble, I asked the boy to rate, on a scale of 0 to 10, how "grown up" he felt at school — he was quick to say that he felt "4". I then asked him to imagine that, in a few weeks' time, he came back to see me and answered the same question by saying that he had reached "9" on the scale. I asked him to describe what he would be doing differently when he had reached 9, what his teacher would notice about him, how he would be responding to frustrations, and so on. After some hesitancy, he began to elaborate more and more excitedly what being "9" would be like and developed a comprehensive picture of that (future) solution state. It was then possible to suggest that he "practice" some of the particular behaviours he had nominated, behaviours that were part of being "9" on the grown-up scale.

Whereas a problem-focused approach points back to the past, a solution-focused approach is inherently future-oriented. It is grounded in the idea that there will be a time when the effects of the [problem] are no longer dominating. It can be helpful to invite clients explicitly to focus on the future and consider how the discoveries they are making might make a difference. (Durrant & Kowalski, 1990, p. 98)

I will discuss later the use of the "miracle question", and of "scaling questions", which provide a description of what the solution-state WILL be like — and so provide concrete goals to work towards in counselling.

3   ASSESSMENT

I have sometimes commented that it amazes me what people think psychologists know — the only thing that amazes me more is what some psychologists think psychologists know! This is not a glib statement, but reflects my concern about the "special knowledge" that is assumed, particularly in that activity known as "assessment".

How does "assessment" fit with an approach that utilises the ideas presented in this book? At first glance, it might seem that the two are incompatible.

Of course, in talking about any supposed incompatibility, I am not referring to assessment that is primarily educational, that seeks to identify a particular focus for remedial intervention (although, even then, we must remember both that the process of assessment has an effect on the student's beliefs about him/herself and that the way that any intervention is framed can make a difference).

However, when considering assessment that precedes counselling or therapy, it is important to consider how the process of assessment fits with the assumptions that underlie our work. There is often a request, overt or covert, that counsellors *assess* a troublesome student *in order that* school personnel will know how best to deal with him or her. Clearly, this request reflects a particular (and very common) assumption about therapy — that detailed information about the problem, its history, its incidence, and so on, leads to discovering its solution.

Psychological assessment

- assumes that psychological or emotional qualities exist as measurable entities

- relates to some standard or "normative" criterion for determining health or functionality

- by measuring the characteristics of one person, generally excludes others from the analysis

- seeks assessment information as a basis for planning interventions — assessment identifies "deficits" or weaknesses, which intervention attempts to change or remediate

Brief interactional therapy

- assumes that the meaning of behaviour and emotion is relative

- proposes that psychological and emotional characteristics are as much a product of the observer's interpretation or assessment as they are of the characteristics of the person

- seeks to include the responses of others in the analysis

- suggests that intervention may not be related directly to the problem

- seeks to build on strengths and resources rather than repair deficits.

In contrast, O'Hanlon and Weiner-Davis suggest:

> It is usually unnecessary to know a great deal about the complaint in order to resolve it.
>
> Typically, solution-oriented therapists do not find it useful to gather extensive historical information about the presenting problem. Sometimes, only a bare minimum of information is necessary to begin resolving the complaint. We have found that therapists often get stuck because they have too much information rather than too little, or too much information about the problem and too little about the solution. (1989, p. 38)

Berg (1991) discusses the fact that "assessment" and "treatment" are intertwined. One of the greatest dangers of assessment is NOT whether or not we do it, but that we might believe that it is somehow separate from the process of counselling. That is, our assessment involves interaction with the student and thus has some impact on later interactions.

Berg comments that assessment often results in a "laundry list of all the things that are wrong with the client". She comments that this process has an impact on BOTH client and counsellor. I have often thought that one of the reasons that I tend not to gather an enormous amount of assessment data is that I do not want to have the chance to decide that the client is hopeless before I even start. My problem with referral information and assessment information is that I easily become overwhelmed by it. As Berg suggests:

> Once we start to feel overwhelmed by the problems, we tend to look for ways to justify our failure, and so we describe clients as "unworkable", "unmotivated", "lacking insight", "resistive", "shopping around", or "not ready for therapy". (1991, p. 23)

Of course, if we begin to feel overwhelmed by the apparent hopelessness, or even difficulty, of the case, it is extremely likely that we will communicate this to the student, which may either increase the student's sense of hopelessness (if he or she thinks there is a problem) or increase his or her "resistance" (if he or she does not think there is a problem).

Assessing competence

Not only may the assessment of the problem affect the way that we approach counselling, but it also affects the perspective of our client. The very fact of asking questions about the history of the problem, details about when it happens and how terrible are its outcomes, inevitably reinforces a focus on the problem. If people are stuck in thinking their situation unchangeable (as is often the case), then the more we talk about it, the bigger it tends to become.

Hence, an important aspect of assessment from a brief therapy standpoint is assessing strengths, competence, or "exceptions". Often, it is not this straightforward. When students, parents, or teachers have well-formed ideas about the problem and its seriousness, they are not always inclined to respond positively to a focus on competence and exceptions. Parents and teachers, in particular, often expect that we will conduct an exhaustive exploration of every aspect of the situation and our failure to do so may be viewed by them as minimising the situation and so disqualifying their experience of frustration or despair. I have discussed in chapter 4 the importance of our approach "fitting" with the experience of the people with whom we work, and this is just as important in approaching assessment as it is in counselling itself.

However, the major requirement is that they experience us as taking them seriously. It is quite possible to focus on strengths without appearing to dismiss the concerns about the problem.

Assessment information from teachers

Whether our work entails actually counselling the student or only consulting to the teacher, the counselling process begins at the time of referral. The referring teacher is an integral part of the process, since his or her attitudes will have an effect on the way things proceed. If we treat the referral in a way that takes seriously the teacher's concerns, we will better be able to engage the teacher in ways that will enhance the process.

Within the educational system, people are used to forms and protocols. It seems that something that suggests standardisation lends credibility to the

A colleague, who is the Principal of a Special School attached to a specialist child psychiatry unit, often receives detailed information from the school from which a child has come. Children are often admitted to the unit on referral from schools, while others have usually shown difficulties at school (that may or may not be related to the alleged psychiatric problem). The school programme is considered an important part of the therapeutic process, with an assumption that the more individual focus of the Special School will allow educational problems to be addressed in detail. Thus, children's records often arrive with details of tests scores, classroom observations, and so on, seemingly to demonstrate the extent of their problems.

My colleague has begun taking a different stance. Her request to the referring schools is that they provide detailed information about the child's educational strengths. She is concerned to find out what this child is *good at* — which may be particular educational subjects or may be other activities. Her rationale is that a better way to enhance the "self esteem" of these children is to find ways to build on what they can already do well, rather than trying to remediate their deficits. Not surprisingly, as the classroom work focuses on these areas of strength, some children seem to improve in other areas as well. Follow-up advice to the school to which the child later returns focuses on these existing and developing skills, with suggestions of ways to enhance these.

assessment process. Most existing schedules, however, are designed to explore problems and deficits.

Linda Metcalf, from Arlington Texas, has experimented with drafting Teacher Referral Forms that orient the assessment towards competence rather than deficits. These are not complicated and simply formalise the kinds of information that a solution-focused counsellor might seek. An example of such a form is shown on the opposite page — particular situations might require that it be varied.

TEACHER REFERRAL INFORMATION

Name of student: .... Grade: .... Date: ....

Dear teacher,

Thank you for your referral of _____. I am arranging a meeting with the student, and with the parents if that is appropriate. Below, please list the times when you have noticed the student doing BETTER in class. These observations will be very helpful as I try to develop some solutions to the problem you have indicated, since I hope to be able to devise ways to help the student "build on" those (perhaps rare) times that he/she does a little better.

Please return this form to me by _____ .

Please be specific. For example: "Susie does better in class when she is not sitting with her friends and writes down her homework".

1. ....

2. ....

3. ....

4. ....

5. ....

6. ....

7. ....

8. ....

9. ....

10. ....

Teacher's signature: _____

Ron Kral (1989a) has taken the idea of a formal assessment device for eliciting information about competence even further. The "Solution Identification Scale (S-Id)" is a behavioural checklist, a form with which many are familiar, with one important difference. Whilst many checklists and rating forms are ratings of problems or deficits, the S-Id provides ratings of competence or successes. The scale lists positive behaviours, which are rated for frequency of occurrence.

The S-Id has an overtly positive focus, however it does not attempt to ignore problems and difficulties — it still allows raters to indicate that particular behaviours occur "not at all". However, its focus helps orient the process towards an emphasis on strengths. If we ask people to look for deficits, they will usually find them, and their view of the situation will be coloured by this. If we ask people to look for successes, they will usually find them, and their view of the situation will be coloured by this. Thus, the use of the S-Id may help set the assessment and intervention process within a more positive context.

The S-Id is *not* standardised or normed, and so does not result in a "score" that is meaningful in itself. Kral suggests that it "provides a snapshot of possible solutions, positive things which the student is doing or could be doing more often" (1989a, p 9), and so may allow the identification of strengths that have been "hidden" by concerns about the problem. The scale has been used with both teachers and parents, although some items might be omitted from the form if given to teachers, and Kral suggests that the school counsellor should then review the form with the rater.

Discussion of the S-Id ratings might include:

- Comments on the number of items rated "Pretty much" and "Very much".

- Exploration of the behaviours rated "Pretty much" and "Very much" — When do they happen? What is different about those times? What does the parent/teacher do to help make them happen? Which of these might be steps towards building a solution to the current problem?

- Exploration of the behaviours rated "Just a little" and "Not at all"

SOLUTION IDENTIFICATION SCALE (S–Id)

Name: .... Date: .... Rated by: ....

Please answer all questions. Beside each item, indicate the degree to which it occurs.

		Not at all	Just a little	Pretty much	Very much
1	Respectful to grown ups				
2	Able to make/keep friends				
3	Controls excitement				
4	Cooperates with ideas of others				
5	Demonstrates ability to learn				
6	Adapts to new situations				
7	Tells the truth				
8	Comfortable in new situation				
9	Well behaved for age				
10	Shows honesty				
11	Obeys adults				
12	Handles stress well				
13	Completes what is started				
14	Considerate to others				
15	Shows maturity for age				
16	Maintains attention				
17	Reacts with proper mood				
18	Follows basic rules				
19	Settles disagreements peacefully				
20	Gets along with brothers/sisters				
21	Copes with frustration				
22	Respects rights of others				
23	Basically is happy				
24	Shows good appetite				
25	Sleeps OK for age				
26	Feels part of the family				
27	Stands up for self				
28	Is physically healthy				
29	Can wait for attention/rewards				
30	Tolerates criticism well				
31	Can share the attention of adults				
32	Is accepted by peers				
33	Shows leadership				
34	Demonstrates a sense of fair play				
35	Copes with distractions				
36	Accepts blame for own mistakes				
37	Cooperates with adults				
38	Accepts praise will				
39	Able to "think" before acting				
40	COMMENTS :				

From Kral (1989a). Reproduced with permission.

— Which of these will be the first to change? What will be small signs of change in some of these?

Kral comments that he views the S-Id primarily as a clinical tool — that is, in highlighting particular information and designing interventions rather than in obtaining "data" about the child or problem.

Assessment with students

If our work with students is oriented towards change then the most useful part of the assessment process is the clinical interview. Since our concern is with how students view themselves and the situation, we can best discover, and influence, this through our interaction with them.

Linda Metcalf has used a form, similar to the Teacher Referral Form shown earlier, to encourage students to identify their strengths and exceptions. The form is the same as the teacher's form, with the initial information altered.

STUDENT INFORMATION SHEET

Name of student: .... Class: .... Date: ....

Dear student,

Your teachers and I are interested in assisting you here at school. Below, please list the times you think you do better in school. This is your chance to tell us what you think will help you do well here at school.

Please be specific. For example, "I do better in school when I think the teacher likes me, when I understand the homework, when I get to see my Dad, etc."

Linda has used this form successfully is school settings, although I can imagine that some students would not feel comfortable filling out a form, or might think it "dumb". Certainly, if something of this kind is used, it should either be completed jointly with student and counsellor, or be discussed with the student soon afterwards. She usually gives a copy of both the completed student form and the completed teacher form to the parents, and may suggest that parents and student review these together.

A less formal approach may begin, in the interview situation, simply by asking "What do you think it would be helpful for me to know about your situation?" (particularly for students who have sought counselling) or "What do you think I should know about why your teachers thought you should see me?" That is, we begin by finding out what the student thinks is pertinent rather than with some predetermined list of assessment areas. As I have discussed, it is quite likely that the student will have a different "agenda" from that of the referring teacher — and it is his or her own agenda about which the student is most likely to be motivated. Hence, it is important that we do not begin by using the teacher's complaints or concerns to beat the student over the head, but see the "assessment" phase as one in which to gain some understanding of how the student sees things.

A school counsellor was concerned that the processes that occurred around a student's suspension from school helped confirm people's views of the student as a problem and so affected the chances of the student even being able to make a "fresh start" at a new school.

She devised a procedure for obtaining information on students whose suspension was definite — explaining to teachers that she needed information, in as much detail as possible, about any strengths or successes the student had shown, so that she could pass this information on to the new school. This would help them gain a more balanced picture, not only of the student but also of the school from which he had come.

THE QUICK INTERVIEW FOR KIDS

Ron Kral, a school psychologist in Milwaukee, was a faculty member at the Brief Family Therapy Center. He has given much thought to the relationship between his "solution focus" in his therapeutic work and the demands of assessment as a school psychologist.

The "Quick Interview for kids", or Q.I.K. (Kral, 1989b), is a protocol for assessment that is geared towards a solution-focused approach to therapy. That is, it is not designed to obtain information for diagnosis or explanation, but is designed to be used in counselling with students in such a way as to provide a direction for therapy.

That is, the QIK is more concerned with how the student sees him or herself, and with providing information about what the student's solution will be like, than with information that helps locate the student on some normative scale.

Question 1	Think about the best person (student, brother/sister, friend, worker, etc.) you could be — the ideal you. Make sure it is possible and give that person 100 points. Now, tell me how many points you would give yourself these days.
Question 2	On a scale of 1 to 10, now rate how much you like (or how satisfied you are with) your rating on the previous 1 to 100 scale.
Question 3	When you move from '60 to 70' (or '85 to 90', etc.) what will be different which will tell you that things have changed? ... Have you been at '70' (or '90', or ...) before, and if so what was happening then? ... What is the highest you have ever been on the scale? When — what was going on then?
Question 4	What are the chances that you could ... (do the exception) ... again (or now)?

Kral explains the four questions in the following way:

Question 1 — This question provides an estimate of "self-concept" in the sense of a client's feelings of "measuring up" to some standard. It is self-anchored in the sense that the therapist has no idea of what the numbers represent at this point. An informal survey with adults, however, suggests that the most "normal" people rate themselves anywhere from 70 to 85.

Question 2 — This question is more like "self-esteem". While you can have a certain concept or rating of yourself, your opinion or value of that may vary. Kids who are highly satisfied may not be good "customers" (de Shazer, 1988) since they tend to be satisfied with the status quo. However, this is only a guess or working hypothesis which will need to be tested later. The question does provide a sense of initial investment.

Question 3 — de Shazer (1988) discusses the "Miracle Question" which is used to help define potential solutions without focusing on the problem. These questions are another way of doing this along with opening the door for defining potential exceptions (instances when success was occurring already or the conditions which the kid defines as successful). In addition, you can begin to help the child form intermediate goals (what things will be like in 5 or 10 points, not when the final solution is attained). Follow-up enquiry to these questions is crucial to help clearly and behaviourally define what the kid will be doing, thinking and feeling differently. Responses which provide exceptions based on things which someone else or divine providence need to provide are not acceptable since the client will be asked deliberately to act on those parts of the exception pattern which are under his/her control.

Question 4 — Here you are indirectly hinting that the exception is important AND should be done. Similarly, by obtaining a rating which could be a scale from 1 to 10 or some description ("pretty good", "excellent" or "fat chance!"), you have another estimate of commitment and pave the way to assign the exception as a task.

Rather than being constrained by notions of "norms", Kral comments that the questions can be elaborated on as needed in each case. Hence, he is more concerned with understanding how *this* student sees him or herself than with rating the student on some "independent" scale.

(From Kral, 1989b — reprinted with permission)

ASSESSMENT FOR INTERVENTION

Within the brief therapy approaches, the role of assessment is to provide sufficient information to allow intervention. That is, our concern is with what to *DO* about the problem, how to make things different, rather than with *WHY* it is happening.

A solution-focused counsellor may spend very little time exploring the problem — preferring to "assess" successes and "exceptions". A counsellor using ideas such as those from the MRI may seem to focus more on the problem — however the aim of assessment is still primarily pragmatic.

Murphy (1992, p. 63), based on Fisch *et al* (1982), suggests that an initial assessment focus on five aspects of the situation:

i.   The specific nature of the problem

ii. Previous and current solution attempts

iii. Minimal goals of the client

iv. Client's "position" (client's beliefs and values about the problem)

v.   Chief complainants (who is most interested in resolving the problem?)

Cade and O'Hanlon (1993), reviewing the various brief therapy approaches, suggest the following list of questions for assessment:

i.   When does the problem occur?

ii. Where does the problem occur?

iii. What is the performance of the problem? (That is, what does it "look like")

iv. With whom does it occur?

v.   What are the exceptions to the rule of the problem?

vi. What does the client or clients do differently, or what do they stop doing, because of the problem?

vii.   What do the clients show in the session that is related to the problem?

viii. What are the clients' explanations and frames regarding the problem?

ix.   What are the client's or others' attempted solutions regarding the "problem"?

x.   How will we know when we get there?

The concern of both lists is with obtaining information to assist in formulating interventions.

Some important aspects seem to be:

1.   Describing the problem specifically & behaviourally

Brief therapy does NOT deny emotion. In fact, if our concern is with the experience of the people with whom we work, we cannot possibly deny emotion. What characterises brief therapy is its view of the place of emotion in therapy — that is, a belief that the expression of emotion does not necessarily bring about change. Also, as Cade and O'Hanlon (1993) point out, descriptions of emotion are generally attributions based on the experience of behaviour. Thus, we tend to focus on the observable.

> While feelings and thoughts are viewed as important, behavior is viewed as the bottom line in the family therapy of MRI. It is only through behavior that affective and cognitive experiences and events are manifested. (Bodin, 1981, P. 292)

Counselling is a complicated enough activity, and it helps if all present know that they are talking about the same thing! If the description of the problem is "She has low self-esteem", we cannot be sure that we are all operating on the same idea of what "low self-esteem" is. However, if the problem is described as "She cries when she makes a mistake in her work", our focus is less ambiguous. We may be able to make a difference to this behaviour, even if we never address "self esteem" explicitly. Similarly, "he is angry all the time" is not as useful as "when corrected in class, he closes his book and refuses to do any more work".

O'Hanlon and Wilk (1987) use the idea of "video descriptions," which encourage specific descriptions of what is (or, will be) happening. Their idea is that we should obtain the kinds of information that we would get if we were to watch a videotape of the problem behaviour or situation. To quote the 60s detective, "Just wanna get the facts" — everyone's interpretations about motivation or emotion just get confusing.

2. Describing the interactional sequences around the problem

The MRI approach seeks to help people "do something different". In order to do this, we need to know what people are doing.

I have suggested that parents and students and/or teachers and students tend to become stuck in repetitive sequences of behaviour around a problem, and that these sequences often inadvertently help perpetuate the problem. Intervention may require suggesting that one party do something that is different from the usual sequence, or reframing the problem in a way that allows something to occur that is not part of the usual sequence, or focussing on something that is already occurring that is not part of the usual sequence. Thus, it may be helpful to know what the usual sequence is. This complements the previous suggestion about specific, behavioural descriptions, since information about sequences tends to be more specific than vague problem "names".

For example, a description of a problem such as "school refusal" or "school phobia" is not only very general and vague, it also does not include information about the interactional pattern. An exploration of what happens, who does what, and when, in relation to the child's refusal to go to school, may yield important information about something small that could be changed. Advising parents that "you need to take a tough stance" may not be helpful — in the light of their frustration and despair, it may appear impossible. However, a thorough exploration of the sequence of behaviour may show that child gets up, watches TV, parent calls her for breakfast, child eats breakfast, parent asks "How are you feeling about school today", child's attitude changes, parent begins to encourage, child refuses to get dressed, parent pleads, child complains of feeling sick ... and so on, provides more useful information about where an intervention may be directed. Advising the parent to insist on "no TV and no breakfast before you are in your school uniform" is more manageable, but may be sufficient to interrupt the pattern that has become entrenched. Even something small, such as asking the parent to experiment with NOT asking "How are you feeling about school today", is achievable but may make a significant difference.

3.   Describing attempted solutions

This fits well with the previous point, since much of what people DO to try to solve the problem is reflected in the interactional patterns that occur. Thus, it can be important to obtain information not only about what happens around the problem, but also about what people do to try to deal with, or solve, it.

For example, parents' repeated lectures may be not working, however they are their genuine attempts to solve the situation.

Discipline is usually an attempt to solve a problem of unacceptable behaviour. At times, when a situation has seemed to become intractable, repeated imposition of detention may actually be serving to perpetuate the problem. An analysis of this attempted solution may allow the counsellor both to validate the teacher's intention in imposing more and more punishment, and also suggest a different response — a response which might not immediately "make sense", but which might lead to a different response.

Craig (1987) has described a case of a fifth grade boy, with a history of behaviour problems, who was refusing to attend school, where an assessment of the attempted solutions suggested that the school system had inadvertently become part of the problem.

> A solution the school had employed was to involve a Home/School Liaison Officer (HSLO) to ensure an acceptable degree of attendance ... When the HSLO was able to "catch"

William he was brought to school. William was not required to take any responsibility for his attendance, therefore this attempted solution inadvertently participated in the development of William's bad habits. (Craig, 1987, p. 9)

A small change in the pattern — whereby the HSLO's role was framed as "assisting the parents, when they requested assistance" (rather than usurping the parents), and later as "coaching the student" (rather than taking control) — was sufficient to make a difference

Of course, this does NOT mean that the solution of someone, such as an HSLO, forcing a student to school is always unhelpful. In some situations, it may become unhelpful — usually if it is repeated even though it is not working. In this particular case, the attempted solution had become part of the stuck pattern.

4. Describing the client's "position"

Whilst we tend not to look for "causes" for problems (since, even if we could discover them, we could not necessarily do anything about them — certainly not quickly, with the constraints of school pressures), we may be interested in what the student, or parents, or teacher sees as the cause of the situation, since this will affect their stance regarding counselling and their apparent "motivation". The way that the people with whom we work make sense of the problem and what it means will determine their attitude to our counselling. (For example, if parents think of their child's problems as being "A.D.D", they are less likely immediately to appear cooperative with counselling that is non-medical — thus, we will have to frame the situation in a way that enhances their cooperation.)

Within the brief therapy field, several people have described the notion of "customership" for counselling. This idea was introduced by the MRI Brief Therapy Project (Fisch et al., 1982) and has been adapted by de Shazer and his colleagues (de Shazer, 1988). Rather than thinking in terms of "motivation" or "resistance," this idea seeks to describe the different positions clients present in relation to a particular problem. (See opposite page for a summary of these descriptions).

VISITORS, COMPLAINANTS and CUSTOMERS

A **visitor** (defined also by Fisch, et al, 1982 as a "window shopper") is uncommitted, often involved in therapy under some kind of duress, implicit or explicit, and usually because of the concerns of others. However clear it may be to those others or to us that this person has problems, he or she has no agenda to talk, in the current context, about problems or to receive help. Any attempt at intervention is, therefore, likely to be fruitless or to lead to what could subsequently be called "resistance". Steve de Shazer's advice in such situations is respectful listening, compliments where possible, but no tasks (de Shazer, 1988).

A **complainant** has a particular complaint (or list of complaints), specific or vague, either concerning themselves or about some other person(s) and about which they are usually prepared to talk, sometimes at length. However, although they may either see themselves as being relatively powerless, or as having the potential to influence the problem(s) through their own actions, it is not yet clear that the therapist is being invited directly to offer help to them (or they may take the position that it is up to the other person(s) to change, not them, in which case they should probably be treated initially as a visitor, with empathy, but no tasks given).

A **customer** is someone who comes in with a complaint, about themselves or about some other person(s), of which it is possible to gain a relatively clear description, and about which he or she quite clearly wishes to do something for which the therapist's help is being sought.

It is important not to see these definitions as describing fixed and real "characteristics" of clients, but purely as guidelines for thinking about the therapy relationship. They describe positions adopted by clients in relation to the positions, or the anticipated positions, taken by therapists, and by other family members or professionals involved. It is also common for members of a family to adopt different positions vis-à-vis each other, and also to vary in the positions they adopt both within a session or from one session to another.

This summary of the descriptions "visitor, complainant, and customer" is from an unpublished handout by Brian Cade, and is reproduced with his permission.

Counselling is most likely to be cooperative and effective when the focus is on something for which the client is a "customer".

Students referred to counsellors may often be seen as "visitors" — they do not tend to invite teachers and counsellors to help them change, and they often do not agree with other's view of the problem. Therefore, their apparent lack of motivation is perfectly understandable. However, "customership" (or "visitorship") is not a characteristic of the person but is a way of describing the counsellor-client interaction. de Shazer talks of these terms as "code words" and explains that, "the code word 'customer' ... describes a therapist-client relationship, *as a result of the interview*, that is built on the client's wanting to do something about building a solution" (de Shazer, 1988, p. 42 — italics added). By the end of an interview, the counsellor and student may have constructed a different definition of the situation — a different agenda — and the student may be a "customer" for that.

Assessing "position" allows us better to decide where to focus our intervention. For example, if parents are not really concerned about a situation, then we are more likely to be effective if we focus on the student and perhaps the teacher, rather than wasting time and energy trying to "motivate" them.

When counsellors find themselves getting stuck with a particular student, closer examination often shows that the counsellor is working harder (is more invested in the outcome) than is the student. Not only is this situation exhausting — it just doesn't work (or, it requires that the counsellor adopt a "social control" stance rather than a therapeutic one). A useful way to avoid getting stuck is constantly to think about "who is the customer, and for what?". When it is the counsellor who is the customer for change (perhaps because the school system demands this), rather than the student, then it is time to do something different — renegotiate the problem to enhance the student's "customership", or focus the intervention elsewhere.

5.   Describing exceptions, and minimal goals

As described above, one of the aims of assessment is to assess strengths and competence rather than problems and deficits.

Thus, an important part of our assessment is to obtain information about when the problem is NOT happening, as well as information about the sequences that occur when it does happen. In terms of assessment, it is important to remember that information about exceptions is not just something that we think about AFTER the initial assessment of the problem, but is an integral part of our initial data-gathering. As discussed above, the fact of our asking about exceptions or strengths from the outset may affect the direction in which our counselling or intervention proceeds.

In my own work, I try to be alert to possible exceptions from the very beginning of my contact with clients. In the case example in chapter 9, the therapist (Kate Kowalski) is met with a passionate elaboration of the problem from the mother. In the midst of this, mother says, "One day she'll be very good in class ... and then there will be days on end where she just will not do anything." Kate responds by asking about those days when "she will be very good in class". That is, she was alert to any indication of exceptions early in the interview.

Had she been concerned to "assess" the problem, this potential exception would have been missed. However, it became an important basis for orienting the rest of the interview around already existing examples of competence. Once the interview had begun to explore the student's success, the precise details of the problem became less important.

Rather than asking, "Are there ever times when this doesn't happen?", it is usually preferable to ask "When was the *last* time that this didn't happen?" The latter question implies that exceptions are occurring and so the client is more likely to remember them.

Kral (1988) outlines his "5'D' Process" for assessment and intervention design:

1. **D**evelop an image of a realistic solution
2. **D**iscover how and in what ways the solution is already in action
3. **D**etermine small measurable steps (goals) towards the solution
4. **D**escribe those thoughts/feelings/actions which can be useful in attaining the goals
5. **D**o something to make a difference

Here, formulation of goals and identification of exceptions are linked. Goals are discussed initially in terms of "what will the solution be like?". This picture is made more real by asking about those times it is already (even in a small way) in action — exceptions. On the basis of what has already happened, it is then possible to describe small, manageable and observable steps which will lead towards the goals. Since these are small, students can usually describe what they *will be doing/thinking/feeling* when these steps are happening. Intervention flows naturally from this — and may amount to little more than doing something different (practising one of the small steps, or stopping doing something that isn't working).

If assessment has any practical use, it is in helping formulate goals for intervention. From a brief therapy perspective, assessment is an integral part of intervention rather than being something that "measures" something for its own sake. The aim of assessment is to discover where therapy is heading. This is what Cade and O'Hanlon mean by their inclusion in the list of assessment areas, "How will we know when we get there?".

6. Scaling problems and solutions

The QIK shown earlier utilises the idea of having students "scale" their situation — rate themselves on a scale from 1 to 10. As Berg & Miller (1992) comment:

> There is magic in numbers. When the client is asked to put his problems, priorities, successes, emotional investments in relationships, and level of self-esteem on a numerical scale, it gives the therapist a much better assessment of the things he has to know. ... the scaling questions are designed to inform the therapist and are also used to motivate, encourage, and enhance the change process." (pp. 82–83)

Scaling questions are of the form:

On a scale from 0 to 10, where 10 means how you want things to be, and 0 means the worst things have been, where would you say you are right now?

My experience has been that clients, from children to adults, are almost always able to answer this question meaningfully.

Of course, the question in itself has no great value — it all depends on how it is used. First, it all depends on how the scale is described. As with any other question/intervention, the description of the scale needs to FIT.

- On a scale of 0 to 10, where 0 is "I'll never be able to stay out of trouble in class", and 10 is "I know I can keep myself out of trouble", where would you put yourself at the moment?

- On a scale of 0 to 10, where 0 is being not grown up at all, and 10 is being really grown up (for your age), where would you say you are?

- On a scale of 0 to 10, where 10 is "I'll do anything to resolve this situation", and 0 is "No, I don't think I can be bothered", where would you put yourself at the moment?

- On a scale of 0 to 10, where 0 is "I don't feel like I can do any of my school work", and 10 is "I feel pretty well on top of my work", how would you rate where you are?

The answers to scaling questions are completely self-referenced — they do not relate to external criteria. It is not uncommon to find that parents and child, or student and teacher, rate the student differently. That is okay, for it leaves open the possibility of exploring what will be different when the two ratings agree.

Further, scaling questions are not static. As Kowalski and Kral (1989) suggest:

> ... the scale builds on the assumption of change in the desired direction. Since a scale is a progression, the number '7' assumes the numbers '10' as well as '5', '3', or '1'. It also assumes movement (or change) in one direction or another, rather than stagnation. By virtue of this, an expectation of change is built into the process of asking scaling questions. (p. 61)

In themselves, scaling questions are useful, since they allow clients "to visualize or imagine, in a very natural way, [their] experiences as the numbers on the scale are representative of them" (Kowalski & Kral, 1989, p.

60). However, these questions may then provide a "platform" for asking about exceptions.

> *Okay, so you say you are '5' on that scale of "feeling self-control" now. What's the highest you've ever been? When was that? What were you doing then? How did that make things different?*

By asking about the highest the student has ever been (a question that assumes there has been such a time), we are likely to gain information about previous exceptions to the problem. If these have happened before, maybe they can happen again. An exploration of WHAT the student was doing differently at the time, and HOW it made things different, begins to build a picture of the student doing things differently — and the possibility of doing (even some of) it again becomes a more real possibility.

Scaling questions may also provide a means for adopting a future focus.

> *Yes, it sounds right that you are '3' on the scale of "getting on with work". Let's just imagine that you come back to see me in a couple of weeks and you tell me that you have moved to '5' on that scale. What will be happening differently then? What will you have done to move yourself from '3' to '5'?*

This is similar to the "miracle question", which gives a detailed picture of the solution state. The advantage of this form of the future focus is that it envisages a future of smaller steps towards success. For some, it is easier to envisage moving from '3' to '5' or '6' than to imagine moving to '10'.

I sometimes comment to clients that changing is like climbing a mountain. If you are climbing the south face of Everest, you don't keep looking at the summit. In the midst of the climb, if you keep looking up at the top, you are likely to fall off! From what I know of mountain climbing (I've watched TV documentaries), climbers concentrate on the next step — the next place to put their foot, or the next place to tie their rope.

In the same way, scaling questions can help make small steps (the "minimal goals" of the last section) seem meaningful and, perhaps, achieveable. The important thing is that the minimal goals (what *was* happening, or what *will* be happening) are described in concrete detail.

With children, the scale can be made more concrete in various ways. This might be by drawing a line on a blackboard, or by describing it differently and more graphically. Cade & O'Hanlon (1993, p. 108) describe examples of the scale being explained differently.

> "If this single brick stands for when you are being very noisy in class and behaving like a five-year-old, and this tall pile of bricks stands for when you have been able to behave like a ten-year-old, what size of pile would stand for how grown-up you have been this last few days?"

> "If this small circle on the blackboard shows me how shy you used to be, and this big circle shows me how brave you are going to be, draw me a circle to show me the bravest you have been this week."

Scaling questions can also be useful to gauge the client's impression of change between sessions — either by reference to a previous scaling answer, or by describing the scale as "where you were last time" and "where you are now". Often, clients who seemed despondent about progress "discover" that they are doing better than they thought when asked to scale their relative positions.

> In a case with a Year 6 girl who was experiencing what some would call an "obsessive-compulsive" problem, I had reframed the situation as "the fears pushing you around" and had spent a couple of sessions focusing on exceptions. In the third session, it was clear that things were much better however Sarah did not seem to appreciate this. She acknowledged that she had had a number of "victories" over the fears, but this was not seeming to lead to a generally more hopeful outlook. Rather than continue to focus on specific incidents of success, I asked her to "rate" the power of the fears previously and now.

Michael: So you think they're getting pretty angry? They've discovered that you're getting bigger than them, and they're getting smaller than you?

Sarah: Yes

Michael: When you first came to see me, how big did you think they
were and how big did you think you were?

Sarah: I didn't think about them that way.

Michael: No, but thinking about it now, how big do you think they
were and you were back then?

Sarah: I was pretty small compared to them ... they were like as
big as a giant.

Michael: Like were they sort of this big *(indicates level with his
shoulder)*, or this big *(stands up)* or this big *(stands on
chair)*?

Sarah: They were ... um, like a giant.

Michael: Oh, so they were bigger than this *(Points to ceiling)*.

Sarah: Yes

Michael: And how big were you? Compared to them ...

Sarah: I was my size

Michael: So, if they were that big, how big were you in relation to
them?

Sarah: Like as big as me sitting down here.

Michael: So you were about there *(points to her shoulder)*, and they
were about there *(jumps)*

Sarah: Yes

Michael: Show me where you think they are now.

Sarah: *(Moves her hand about 10 cm off the floor)*

Michael: There?

Sarah: Yep

Michael: Really!

Sarah: Yes

Michael: And show me how big you are now in relation to them

Sarah: As big as I am when I'm standing up.

Michael: Stand up and show me.

We marked Sarah's height on the whiteboard, sitting and stand-ing, and indicated the "before-and-after" heights of the fears. It was clear that the change was evident to Sarah, and the small stature which she afforded them was impressive. I was particularly interested in her choosing the change in her own relative height as being from her height sitting to her height standing. I had, once or twice, used the term "standing up to the fears" in my questions and commented now that Sarah seemed to be saying that she had truly stood up to them.

(Durrant, 1989, pp. 27–28)

Kowalski & Kral (1989) comment that it is a matter of personal style whether the therapist describes the "worst" scenario as being '10' or '0' on the scale. Berg (1991) suggests that "culturally (at least in western society) we tend to view 10 as bigger, better and higher than 1 ... Therefore, the most desirable state is placed at 10". My preference is to describe the scale such that the desired (or goal) state is '10' — so clients can "see" progres-sion towards the solution.

If a child has behaviour problems, it is because they are too dull or too bright to manage the regular program at school. Psychological testing is generally requested to investigate this claim. In current practice, the amount of time spent by psychologists doing individual assessments exceeds that of time spent on any other activity. Individual assessments have emphasised linear perspectives of problems with children at school. When an individual assessment is made, it is assumed either consciously or unconsciously, that the problem lies within the individual child. ... While it is acknowledged that a psychological assessment may be required for some cases, in the majority of situations the assessment only adds more data to a student's file which has no use. Thus, psychological assessment needs to be seen as a last resort rather than the first line of intervention. (Brown, 1986, p. 15)

4   FEELING HEARD

After I had asked the foster parents of one adolescent about times
when his behaviour was different, they commented desperately, "Yes,
that's right. Sometimes, he *deliberately* behaves himself at school —
just to upset us!" This was not an expression of their covert "rejec-
tion", or of their "unwillingness to change", but rather a reflection of
their feelings of hopelessness. My questioning of exceptions had not
fitted with the foster parents' experience of their situation and so
seemed to them that I was trying to "convince" them that things were
better than they thought. I had failed to "validate" their experience of
failure and so appeared to be minimising the seriousness of the
problem.

Our aim in counselling, particularly counselling based on a solution-
focused, or competency-based, perspective, is to develop a co-operative
relationship with the person with whom we are working. Nothing in the
principles of brief therapy contradicts what we all already know about the
counselling relationship.

*Anything we do in counselling is wasted, if our clients do not
feel that their experience of the situation has been validated.*

As Cade and O'Hanlon point out:

> It is our belief that clients usually only hear when they feel
> that they have been heard, when their experiences have been
> validated, including their affective experiences. We believe
> that a therapist, of whatever school of therapy, must pay suffi-
> cient attention to this aspect of a client's experiences for any
> therapy to be effective. It is in the way that this is done and
> perhaps in the definition of what amounts to'sufficient atten-
> tion' that the various therapeutic approaches differ. The expres-
> sion of feelings is clearly a natural human response and often
> an important one, particularly at crucial moments of grief, joy,
> excitement, fear, etc.. Where therapies often differ is not only
> in the extent to which it is seen as important to acknowledge
> emotions, but also in the extent to which the expression of
> emotions is believed to play a crucial and central role in the
> process of therapy and change. It is our belief, helpful and
> cathartic though explorations and expressions of emotion can
> sometimes be, that the main mechanism of change is through
> the ultimate modification of the constructs through which dis-
> tinctions are made and experience distilled. (1993, pp. 44–45)

Thus, our assessment AND our counselling often involves "walking a
tightrope". On the one hand, we must acknowledge the experience of the
student or teacher to whom we are talking, and validate the experience of
frustration, hopelessness, unfairness, etc On the other hand, we do not want
to focus on the problem to such a degree that we help it seem larger.

Achieving this balance, whilst never easy, can be helped by the direction
we take in our counselling. I will discuss later the issue of "goals" — it is in
this area that we may easily appear to disqualify the experience of the client.

In the brief example above, my questioning about exceptions was
implicitly pursuing the goal of modifying the boy's behaviour. My
assumption was that the foster parents view of his pervasive "bad"
behaviour was affecting their responses, and that these responses
were inadvertently reinforcing his behaviour. Importantly, I was not

seeing them as being "to blame", and I intended also to talk to the boy himself about his behaviour. In hindsight, I am sure that my assumption was "right" — however, it did not fit with their experience. As foster parents, they were committed to trying to make his life as successful as possible and their perceived failure to do this had overwhelming implications for the way they thought about themselves. On the surface, the agenda for therapy was that the boy behave differently. However, his foster parents' view of the hopelessness of the situation (which, interestingly, had been fuelled by other professionals giving them detailed historical information about the boy's abuse and neglect) meant that they saw this agenda as unachievable. Thus, my seeming to pursue it was guaranteed to evoke "yes, but" responses.

At one level, they *were* interested in improving his behaviour (*and their reaction to it*), however their view of the situation meant that (in de Shazer's terms) they were not really "customers" for therapy that focussed on this. I needed to validate their sense of failure and hopelessness. However, this did NOT mean that I ought embark on a lengthy assessment of "how bad things were". To do so might allow them to feel heard but would not change our focus. Rather, it was possible to explore exceptions but to do so in a different way.

"I can see that you have put an enormous amount of time and effort in trying to make things work with Andrew. You seem to have tried everything, and you both sound frustrated that everything you have tried has seemed not to work. What I was wondering was, when was the last time you felt a little less like failures as foster parents."

This question still allowed a focus on more positive aspects of the situation whilst at the same time validating their experience. Gentle exploration of the times they had not so much like failures was a much more useful way of finding out about times they had acted differently and, not surprisingly, some of these times had coincided with improved behaviour on the part of the boy. Simply focusing on when he behaved better did not address their sense of failure. However, focusing on when *they* acted differently allowed them to feel that they had some influence over his behaviour.

5   GOALS — SETTING the AGENDA FOR COUNSELLING

In many approaches to counselling, "goals" are considered important. In situations such as the school setting, where long-term therapy with vague goals (such as "self-awareness") is a luxury we cannot afford, most would agree that therapy should have a clearly-defined goal. However, goals may be thought about in different ways.

> Commonly, goals represent a problem focus. They are framed in terms of "what (problems) the person wants to, or needs to, work on," "what issues need to be addressed," "what behaviours we need to change," and so on. That is, the goals typically relate to getting rid of some problem or changing some problem situation. No matter how benignly they might be expressed, goals framed in these ways may easily contribute to a continued focus on the problem. However, a continued focus on the problem does not necessarily assist with developing a sense that things can be different for the child or adolescent, for the parents and for the [school] staff. (Durrant, 1993, p. 58)

Rather than focusing on what needs to change or be changed, it may be more helpful to focus on what the changed state will be like — that is, to focus on the nonproblem future. Rather than counselling being driven by ideas about changing whatever problem led to the referral, we might orient things towards what things will be like when the student is ready to finish counselling, to return to class, etc.

As mentioned previously, Cade & O'Hanlon (1993) include in their list of assessment questions, "How will we know when we get there?" They envisage the entire counselling process being "goal driven" rather than "problem driven". This is not just a semantic distinction — it is in the achievement of the goal that lies optimism and feelings of possibility. Lipchik (1988) describes how she often began an initial interview by asking, "How will you know when you don't need to come here any more?" Such a question is loaded with suggestion — it implies that there will be a time when things are better, it implies that the client will be able to be the judge of that, and it implies that the client can imagine that time now.

In an initial therapy session or meeting, these kinds of questions might be used:

- Let's imagine that our talking together turns out to be helpful. What will you be doing differently then?

- It seems like the teachers are on your back alot. Let's imagine that you and I working together convinces them that they can get off your back. How will they know that things are different with you?

- How will you know when you are ready to return to class?

- What will you be doing that will tell you that you are ready to come back to school?

- When you are ready to be part of the class again, what do you think people will notice about you that is different from what's happening now?

- If we made a videotape of you now, and then made another videotape of you when you are not getting in trouble, what will we see that is different on the second video? How will we be able to tell which is the second video?

- How will you know when this student is ready to go back to class?

Not only do questions such as these establish a focus on future success rather than on past failure, they also help the goals be described in concrete terms. They all include the notion, "What will you/he/she be doing when things are better?" Vague goals ("I will be behaving better") are hard to measure and hard to achieve. Since we could always find more ways to "behave better," it is possible that the student, or the parents, or the school staff, may never be confident that the goals have been reached. The more that goals seem ephemeral, the more the person feels like "No matter how much I achieve, there is always another step," and so the more likely it is that students will give up. de Shazer (1988) points out that concrete goals, which provide a sense of "how we will know when we get there," are an important step towards promoting the possibility of a solution and will often help clients recognize that some of what is needed is already happening.

How will you know when things are better?

Moves the focus from the problem (or what people have thought of as the problem) to the solution.

Is more hopeful, and so might lead to more cooperation.

Yields descriptions of behaviour that WILL be happening.

The achievement of these specific behaviours becomes the goal.

Leads to questions about when these are already happening.

Questions about the solution state allow us to obtain information about specific behaviour. Of course, initial answers may be given in terms such as "they won't be hassling me", and may require further exploration. What we want to know is "what will be different when they are not hassling you?" — which might be, "I will not hide in the library at lunchtime", followed by "How will that make things different for you?" — "I will be able to talk to the guy in Year 9 who has a computer" — and counselling might then work towards being able to talk to that student.

Goals formulated in this way are more likely to be meaningful, measurable and achievable. They may lead to an exploration of times when the desired behaviours are *already* happening (since it is quite likely that there have already been times when the student has talked to the student in

Year 9, even if he cannot think of times he has felt less hassled), or to small steps towards managing this behaviour.

In my work in residential care settings, such goals often become a kind of a "theme" that permeates the entire placement. For example, my colleagues in an acute psychiatric hospital near Washington, D.C., ask questions along the lines of "how will you know when you are ready to be discharged?", and then seek to respond to everything that happens during the admission in reference to this. Other residential programmes develop a "theme" based on the goals, such as "getting in control of my life", elaborate specific things that will be indicators of achieving this. and then use the language of the theme consistently.

In residential settings, achieving the goal is the basic reason for being there, so it makes sense to refer to it regularly. However, students are not at school primarily to achieve particular therapeutic goals and so it may not be appropriate that "goal language" be used so pervasively. Nonetheless, when a student has been identified as a problem, it may be possible for some staff to respond to his or her behaviour, at least for a time, in terms of "we noticed you doing something today to help you be able to return to class", and so on.

Future certainty vs. future possibility

The language we use is important, since it conveys all sorts of subtle cues that will either help or hinder the movement towards the goal.

In exploring goals, using the kinds of questions suggested above, it is helpful to use phrases such as "What WILL you be doing WHEN this is no longer a problem?" rather than "What WOULD you be doing IF this was no longer a problem?".

"Future certainty" language conveys the suggestion that things WILL get better. Erickson's hypnosis work used "suggestion" a great deal — using language to *suggest* ideas and outcomes, rather than specifying them overtly. In a similar way, language that suggests that change will occur helps orient the client towards the expectation of change. It's like saying, "I know you will be able to achieve this", without saying it!

Whose goals?

When students appear to be unmotivated, it is often the goals that are the problem. We are all most likely to be motivated to work towards goals that we have set and are therefore meaningful for us, and least likely to be motivated to work on goals imposed by someone else. One of the least fruitful activities in which we can engage is to try to convince a student that he or she has a particular problem. Just because a teacher, or the school executive, or parents have identified what the problem is and what needs to happen does not mean that the student will agree. (Paraphrased from Durrant, 1993, p. 64)

My experience is that the people with whom we work usually want things to be better. It is just that we must understand what they mean by "better," not what we assume they mean — and, we have to put aside our ideas about whether what they mean by "better" seems reasonable to us or not.

Other people's problem

Students are often referred to counsellors without being extremely willing. If the choice is counselling or suspension, counselling is (only just) a better option. However, it is not surprising that they arrive at the counsellor's office unmotivated, and suddenly seem to have a vocabulary that consists entirely of "Nuh" and "Dunno".

As I have said above, trying to convince them that they have a problem is a sure recipe for counsellor frustration. Rather, we have to find out what it is that *IS* a problem for them.

What we have already said about meaning and behaviour suggests that there is not necessarily a "true" position about what the problem is or what the solution might be. Thus, a pragmatic approach suggests that we will do better by harnessing whatever it is that is the student's motivation, even if it does not accord with what other people want.

In the detailed case example that follows, the school's goal was that the student should acknowledge (confess) his misdeeds and show remorse for his continued misbehaviour, since they felt that this would indicate the likelihood of change. Not surprisingly, the student was not especially interested in showing remorse. However, he WAS concerned that he should not get expelled from school, for this would mean he could not remain on the school's football team. Counselling that focused on his goal of staying on the football team made sense to him and led to ideas about how he might do things differently.

It is easy to get caught up in worrying that change in a student that seems to occur for only "pragmatic" reasons might not be REAL change and might not last. However, ideas about the interactional nature of behaviour suggest that if a student, for whatever reason, begins to behave differently, others will respond to this differently, leading to continued different behaviour in the student, and so on. That is, the very same mechanism whereby interactional patterns may lead to an exacerbation of problem behaviour may also lead to an "exacerbation" of non-problem behaviour.

Thus, whether we think of it as "gaining leverage", "enhancing cooperation", or "utilising motivation", the most useful approach is to focus on what it is that the student wants to be different. This fits with Erickson's "utilization' idea — whatever it is that the student brings, in terms of attitude, beliefs, motivation, etc., we seek to harness this in working towards the solution.

Tiggeman and Smith (1989) describe an approach that cooperates with an adolescent's view that everyone else has an "unfair" view of him or her as a problem, and uses this as a way to encourage the adolescent to do something different "to prove the adults wrong" (See page 62). They describe adolescents who, when the counsellor accepted their view that "it is unfair that the teachers have this view of you", were prepared to behave differently in class "in order to shock the teacher into changing his or her view". They comment that the approach sometimes is even "fun".

The adolescent may not be "motivated" with regards someone else's definition of the problem, however she/he may be "motivated" with regard to a different problem. What is actually a problem to the adolescent? It may be that the fact other people think there's a problem is a problem, or the fact that people are hassling him/her is a problem, or the actions of the teachers/police/parents are a problem — and the adolescent may be interested in trying to do something about one of these.

I have found it useful to accept a child or adolescent's view of the situation and work from that, rather than trying to translate it into terms that fit with what the referrer, or I, think is the problem.

For some adolescents, the problem is that "other people think that there is a problem" and it is most useful to accept this definition and seek to build on it. Thus, the adolescent's goal becomes "proving that I don't have a problem", "getting people off my back", "showing the teachers that I am not irresponsible", and so on. This can lead to a detailed exploration of what will be happening when this goal is reached, getting specific behaviours that the student will be doing, and then enquiring about times these are already happening.

One student did not believe that he had a problem, and the fact that the teacher referred him for counselling was just another example of his being picked on. He was a little sceptical at first, when I suggested that it must be a real hassle having people think he had a problem, and he was not immediately forthcoming when I asked about the effects of this on him. When I persisted with "having teachers think you are a problem is a real problem, isn't it?", he seemed to think I was probably "doing something tricky" — however I persisted and he began to talk about his experience of the situation. After we got passed his initial complaints that it was "unfair", he was able to say that what really got to him about the teachers thinking he was a problem was that they didn't trust him. How was this a problem? — It meant not only that he felt he was being watched all the time, but also that he never got chosen to answer questions in class, to take messages, to do unsupervised activities, and so on.

"What will be happening when the teachers trust you?", I asked, and he mentioned the kinds of activities and privileges that he would be given. "How will these be different?" — he thought that he would enjoy class more because it would not just be the constant drag of work. I explored how this would make a difference for him — he would be happier, he would feel better knowing he was trusted, and if

PROVING TEACHERS WRONG

Jane Tiggeman and Greg Smith (1989) have described what they call "Adolescent shock therapy".

They write about working with adolescents whose view of the problem situation is that it is "unfair" (that narrows it down to about 95% of the students with whom you work!). These are the kids who think they don't have a problem, other people are just giving them a hard time, being on their back or treating them unfairly.

We are all familiar with adolescents who present in this way. Even though we KNOW it will not work, it is all too easy for us to engage in attempts to get the adolescent to "own the problem" — we find ourselves resorting to statements such as "but, surely you can see why your teachers find this annoying?", or "okay, it seems unfair, but think of it from your teacher's point of view", and so on. Our efforts are VERY REASONABLE — to us, but not to the adolescent.

Tiggeman and Smith take the position of agreeing with the adolescent — agreeing that people are giving them a hard time, suggesting that they understand why the adolescent feels fed up. They are not concerned with whether or not this position is "true", however they realize that it might be the only way of gaining the adolescent's trust and cooperation (especially since a student is likely to suspect that the counsellor is just another agent of the school system). They seek to frame the adolescent's motivation in a positive way (without necessarily seeming positive about his or her alleged behaviour). Implicitly, they also reframe the teacher or parent's position in the adolescent's eyes — suggesting that the problem is that the teacher has a mistaken view of the adolescent (as a troublemaker, etc.) rather than the teacher being vindictive.

They talk with the adolescent about how he or she might be able to get the adults involved to change — even though it might seem unfair that the adolescent should have to shoulder this responsibility. Adults are notoriously "thick" and do not change their views easily. Thus, sometimes the adolescent might have to resort to "shock treatment" in order to prove the teachers or parents wrong.

> I started suggesting to Alex that, if he wanted to sort out Miss Nimosa, he could perhaps get her to realize that she was wrong about him, as we both agreed she seemed to see him as a troublemaker. I suggested that maybe he could shock her into realizing that she was wrong. He enjoyed this immensely and he began brainstorming with me ways of shocking her to realize that he wasn't a troublemaker. (p. 10–11).

In their paper, Tiggeman and Smith describe a number of examples of adolescents who went on to be shockingly cooperative, shockingly responsible, shockingly well-behaved, and so on. In each case, this was NOT because the adolescent necessarily thought this the right way to behave, but because he or she saw this as a way to prove the adult wrong. Proving the adult wrong was an agenda, or goal, about which the adolescent was motivated.

Thinking about interactional sequences around problems, it is easy to see that an adolescent doing something different in this way may lead to the adult responding differently. Tiggeman and Smith comment that "the simple fact of the adolescent breaking the impasse opens space for more positive interaction to occur".

he was feeling happier he would get his work finished.

"When was the last time you got your work finished in class?" — he eventually recalled one occasion on which he completed his work, and I continued to find out what was different about that time. His view was that there was one teacher who was not so hard on him, and he tended to be a little more cooperative in her classes. It seemed that perhaps she was someone who did not share the view that he had a problem. I wondered what she was able to notice about him that other teachers perhaps did not see, and he listed a number of small ways in which he behaved differently in her class.

He agreed to keep a secret list, over the next week, of any time he found himself in other classes doing any of the things he usually did in that teacher's class, since these would be the kinds of things that would help him move towards his goal — of showing people that he did not have a problem.

"Unrealistic" goals

What if the goals are unrealistic? It is wise not to be too concerned over that question at the outset. If a student's goal was to return to the same school (even though the school has said it will not have him or her back), and this was pronounced unrealistic, then we can expect little more than "resistance" or defiance. If, however, we accept this goal and explore it further, we will begin to build a picture of things the student might attain. "How will you know when you are ready to return to that school?" or similar questions, may lead to the student specifying particular behaviours or steps towards which he or she wants to work.

As the student works towards these, and school staff respond to them, a different pattern may develop that is more successful. Once the situation has become less stuck, further discussions about the details of his future might open different possibilities (such as other schools). Within the previous context, returning to the old school was the only hope to which she or he could cling. As the student is able to see him or herself differently, we might then be able to discuss other options. That is, once the student has achieved a self-concept of greater success, he or she is more likely to be able to consider other options.

The Miracle Question

de Shazer (1988) describes the "miracle question" as an important part of solution-focused brief therapy and as way for establishing goals that are meaningful for the client.

Suppose one night, while you are asleep, a miracle happens and all the problems that brought you here are solved. How will you know? What will be different that will tell you that the miracle happened? What will your parents/teachers notice that will tell them that it happened?

(paraphrased from de Shazer, 1988, p. 5)

This question, when pursued, leads to a concrete "picture" of what the solution state will be like. Because it is a "let's pretend" question, it makes it easier for people to answer it without becoming bogged down in the "yes, buts" that reflect their current feelings of hopelessness. It is important to explore the answers to the miracle question, to build up as detailed a picture as possible. It is not uncommon for adolescents initially to respond with something like, "They won't be hassling me all the time." Further questioning might proceed along the lines of, "What will they be doing instead? How will that make a difference to you? So, what will you be doing differently? How will that make things different for you? And for them?" and so on. Similarly, when parents identify the miracle as being, "He will be doing what he's supposed to do," we may ask, "So, what are the things he will be doing? How will you respond to that? How will that make things different for you? What will he notice that will tell him that you are pleased?" and so on.

I often say to my students that they should be able to explore the answer to the miracle question for at least twenty minutes. Of course, there is nothing magical about twenty minutes, however it takes time to move from global answers to more specific descriptions of the "miracle state".

The miracle question can have a number of uses. The very fact of developing this detailed description of the solution seems to have the effect of helping people feel that it is achievable. It is almost as if, as the description of the solution is built, the solution becomes a possibility. "It appears that the mere act of constructing a vision of the solution acts as a catalyst for bringing it about" (O'Hanlon & Weiner-Davis, 1989, p. 106). Again, this is much more likely to lead to "motivation". The behaviours that are described as representing the miracle become the goals for counselling.

"YOU CAN'T COME BACK TO SCHOOL UNTIL YOU SHOW REMORSE"

SETTING A MEANINGFUL AGENDA

Colin was in Year 9 at a selective high school. He lived with his mother, step-father and younger sister. Mum and Dad had divorced when Colin was in early primary school, although Dad kept contact. In fact, the school tended to use Dad as the person they contacted in regard to Colin.

After a history of fighting, being disruptive in class, abusing teachers, and persistently failing to do his work, Colin was suspended when he was caught shoplifting on his way home from school (although it was unclear whether the school was more concerned about the shoplifting, or about the fact that Colin was in his school uniform at the time). His suspension was towards the end of term, and he was told that his readmittance to school depended upon his having counselling. Even then, his readmission was not assured.

The school principal expressed the view that Colin was "conduct disordered", and was most concerned that Colin showed no evidence of remorse for his wrongdoings. He said that Colin was involved with a group of teenagers outside the school who were involved in "fringe activities" and this made him pessimistic about Colin's future, particularly, he commented, in the light of his difficult family background. He described Colin as "a persistent liar" and was worried about his influence on other students.

Thus, Colin came to counselling with a formidable list of complaints and a large reputation at school. The "agenda" of the school was that Colin must admit his transgressions, gain some insight into them and their consequences, and show remorse for them. Only then could they have any confidence that he could be managed at school.

Colin was accompanied to the interview by his mother and father (not his stepfather), and my initial thought was that this probably reflected the healthy way in which Dad continued to be involved — a good sign! Unfortunately, this sign soon became completely obscured by Dad's vitriolic attacks on Mum, and on his belief that everyone blamed him for the divorce and so for Colin's problems, and he soon stormed out of the room. As I turned back to Mum, I was greeted with a "see what we have to put up with" expression on her face. Colin, however, maintained his bored expression.

Explanations

If we wanted to speculate on the "causes" of Colin's problem behaviour, there were many possibilities evident even five minutes into the session. For example, we might wonder about the effects on Colin of his parents' divorce and the obvious ongoing conflict. Noting that it was father, rather than stepfather, who came to the interview (despite the fact that stepfather had been with the family for nearly ten years and it seemed that he was fully involved with the children), we might wonder if Colin's behaviour was somehow an attempt to bring Mum and Dad together — and so was perhaps fulfilling some "function" in their ongoing relationship. Alternatively, we might wonder about some "pathology" within Colin, particularly since he seemed so completely lacking in understanding or remorse about his behaviour.

Each of these explanations (and others) may be plausible, and they would each suggest a particular approach that might be followed in counselling. My concern about these explanations is that they all suggest a therapeutic approach that would probably be complex and difficult. Already, it seemed it would be difficult to get Colin's parents to work together on anything. Similarly, the school's view of Colin seemed fairly entrenched and any attempts to resolve the problem using classroom or school programmes were unlikely to be embraced willingly. Finally, I was not confident that Colin was "motivated" to "work on" these problems. Any intervention designed to change him or his behaviour could well be thwarted by his lack of cooperation.

Harnessing "motivation"

After regaining some composure, I asked what the family thought it would be helpful for me to know about their situation. Colin's mother recounted in detail the school's complaints about Colin, adding her feelings that the school had not handled the situation well (an invitation to "take sides", which I thought it best not to hear!). She variously said that he was no real problem at home (so it must be the school's fault — or Dad's), but then that he is defiant and uncooperative at home and fights constantly with his sister. She was clearly frustrated as she said, "I don't know why he keeps doing it. I've talked to him about it. He doesn't seem to realise how important his education is. I just wish he could settle down and get on with his studies."

As she spoke, Colin asserted quietly, "I'm not going to do it any more", however Mum dismissed this with a remark that she had heard that before. I was sure that Colin had probably made such comments many times and it was understandable that people saw them as hollow. It is likely that any such assertions would have been ignored or derided, making the likelihood of their being false almost a self-fulfilling prophecy.

It did not really matter whether or not Colin was being "honest" when he said he was not going to do these things any more. What might be important is that he was making a statement about change. I wondered if I could explore this in a way that might harness, or even create, some motivation on his part.

"Hang on," I interrupted, "what was that, Colin?"

"I'm not going to do it any more."

"What do you mean you're not going to do it any more?"

"Just that. I'm not going to do it any more. But she doesn't believe me."

"Not going to do what any more," I continued (better to stick with statements about change than to get sidetracked onto whether or not Mum believes him).

"You know, all that stuff at school. Telling teachers to get stuffed and mucking up. You now."

"So, you're not going to do it any more?

"No."

"Okay. How come you're not going to do it any more?"

"Cos I'm in the football team", Colin replied.

"Okay, so how does being in the football team mean that you won't do all those other things any more?"

"Well, if I keep getting into trouble, they'll chuck me out of school. And if they chuck me out of school, then I can't stay in the team."

"Oh. So you're not going to do all that stuff any more because you don't ant to get thrown out of school, because you want to stay in the football team."

"Yeah". Colin seemed frustrated that it took me so long to "get it", however I wanted to develop this theme slowly.

We discussed football for a while. My question about whether Colin could just join a different football team led to his explanation that his school's team was among the best and he wanted to stay in it so they could win the district competition again this year.

Motivation?

Football seemed to be one thing about which Colin had some motivation and I thought that there might be a possibility of harnessing this in addressing his behaviour problems. However, it was important that I not seize too quickly on this. Colin's perception had probably been that everyone was "hassling" him about changing his behaviour, and any such hassling was counterproductive. It was important that I not give the impression that I, too, was pressuring him to change. I tried to remain fairly matter-of-fact about his statement, whilst showing that I was taking it seriously.

Can you do it?

"Okay, so do you think you are able to stop doing all this stuff. So you don't get chucked out and can stay in the football team/"

"Yeah. If I want to."

"What helps you be so sure that you can do it?"

"I don't know. I just know I can."

"So staying in the football team is more important that telling teachers off?"

"Yeah."

"And you seem pretty sure that you can do it."

"Yeah."

At this stage, Colin's statement that he would stay out of trouble so he could stay on the football team was little different from similar statements he had probably made before. Nonetheless, it was something about which he was motivated.

Quite apart from his willingness or otherwise to change, my guess was that Colin probably did not really see the possibility of behaving differently. Not only had other people come to expect him to misbehave, but he probably had similar expectations of himself. It might be possible to use his desire to stay in the football team, not as a way to "convince" him to change, but as a means for building a picture of him as capable of behaving differently.

Also, Colin was entertaining changing his behaviour simply as a "means to an end" (staying on the team), rather than as something that was desirable in itself. It was important that I cooperate with this view and not try to convince him that different behaviour was intrinsically better. At the same time, I wanted to elicit information that might provide the foundation for him beginning to think differently about himself.

You've done it before

I discussed with Colin that fact that "not doing it any more" would be difficult. At first, he denied this. However, I continued to review some of the situations in which teachers and/or other students annoyed him and how casy it would be to fall back into the habit of telling them off. I wondered if his desire to stay on the football team was strong enough to allow him to have the kind of self-control that would be required.

"Have there been any other times when you've been able to do something really hard just so you can achieve something that was important to you?"

After some exploration, Colin told me that he used to get sent off quite often when playing football. This was usually because he punched anyone who tackled him "unfairly" and then because he abused the referee if he admonished him. Colin thought his behaviour quite reasonable, however being sent off made it harder for him to score! Scoring was important to him — he was aiming for the award for the most points scored in the season. Eventually, he had decided he had to stop his violence or he would not be able increase his personal score tally.

Again, it was clear that Colin did not change his on-field behaviour because he thought it proper to do so — he continued to believe that other players, and the referee, deserved what he gave them. However, he had changed his behaviour because it did not serve his ultimate ends.

This was not the time for moral judgement on my part. Rather, here was an example of Colin being able to curb his behaviour for a reason that made sense to him. As such, it might provide something on which we could build the idea of behaving differently at school. However, this would not be a matter of, "you did it on the football field so why not do it at school?" Even to imply that would be to risk being seen as yet another exhortation to change. Rather, I wanted to explore Colin's ability to behave differently and so enlarge the picture of him as able to do it.

My questions about, "how were you able to manage this?" initially were met with perfunctory replies. However, as I persisted, Colin remembered (or discovered) that he had found ways both of curbing his frustrations and of expressing them in other ways. This discussion continued for perhaps fifteen to twenty minutes. I wanted to develop the picture of Colin showing self-control in as much detail as possible.

I finished the session by highlighting that I was impressed with Colin's ability to change his behaviour on the football field, although I was still not completely sure how he had managed it. I also commented on how impressed I was not only with his determination to ensure that he did not get expelled from school but also his seeming confidence that he could do it. I wondered what he would do during the holidays to help prepare for this difficult task. I felt it important that I did not explicitly link Colin's self-control on the football field with the required self-control at school, although the link was implicit. My aim was to show that I was taking him seriously without suggesting that I thought he should change his behaviour.

The agenda of the school and others was "insight, understanding and remorse". The agenda that was meaningful to Colin was "not getting chucked out of school". It was important that I stuck to this.

Second session

Two weeks later, Mum reported some signs of Colin being more cooperative at home. I was puzzled at this, since I was not sure how this related to his desire to stay at school. We* tried to highlight these changes in Colin, exploring how he had been able to achieve them, without going overboard in congratulations. His comment was that he had managed to "get Mum off my back a bit". Again, this was Colin behaving differently as a means to an end.

Colin had also been working in his step-father's business during the holidays. Previously, he had not been allowed to do so because he was disruptive and untrustworthy. Again, we wondered about this change and how he had been able to manage it.

The session was largely our being puzzled about these changes and what they might mean, allowing Colin to tell us in detail about what he had done differently. We asked various questions about how he had managed it, what had been hard, when he had been tempted to lose control and how he had managed not to, and so on. As he commented that his changed behaviour made people treat him differently, we commented that he seemed to be someone who "cared about what other people thought", and then that he "cared about what he thought about himself".

The session finished with our wondering how these changes would help

---

*   I was joined for the second and subsequent sessions by Kate Kowalski.

prepare him for the task he was taking on at school.

Subsequent sessions

The third session was similar to the second, in that Mum reported continued improvement in Colin's behaviour at home, commenting that he seemed "more mature". Again, we were careful not to appear too enthusiastic about these changes but spent much time asking Colin about the changes, how he had managed them, and how he made sense of them. His responses suggested that he still saw them largely as a means-to-an-end, although he made a number of comments about how things were "better this way". Tempting though it was to seize on these comments as evidence of a "change in attitude", we felt that to do so would have risked losing him. We wondered what his new views might mean, but continued to focus largely on the "facts" of the changes and exploring their effects.

We highlighted a number of themes that emerged from his answers — "caring more about what he thought about himself", "thinking more about not getting into trouble", and "being able to stick at it".

The fourth session was spent discussing his return to school. We had to provide a report for the school and asked Colin what he thought we should say.

"Tell them to let me come back," was his initial comment. We suggested that it might not be that easy and asked him to explain what we could include in the report that might convince the school to have him back. Thus, the session was spent with us all writing the report together and provided an opportunity for Colin to review all the changes he had made. It was interesting that he described changes in attitude as well as changes in behaviour, and that he saw these as being of interest to the school.

We also discussed with Colin, in a fairly straightforward way, the difficulties of having to contend with his "reputation" and the teachers' expectations that he would not continue any changes, and encouraged him to tell us his plans for dealing with this. When he returned to school, we sought to set up a procedure that would encourage the school to respond to evidence of change rather than just notice any misbehaviour, along the lines set out in the chapter 13).

Did his attitude change?

At no time in this case did we seek to encourage Colin to gain an understanding of his behaviour in a way that might lead to his attitude changing. We did not try to get him to the point at which he would acknowledge that his behaviour had been wrong, or show remorse for it. Rather, we took seriously his very pragmatic view of why he might behave differently.

Some might be concerned that this approach might "reinforce" Colin's attitude, leaving him thinking that his behaviour was acceptable if he had been able to get away with it. Others may be concerned that an approach which did not seek to bring about new understanding would lead only to short-lived, surface changes.

However, Colin was well-practiced at being "immune" to adults' reasoning about why he should change his ways. Had it seemed that our agenda was the same as that of the school and others, he would most likely have maintained a "defiant" stance and therapy would have been a contest. Our rule of thumb was that counselling with any client is only likely to be successful if the agenda is that which is meaningful to the client, regardless of what others might think of it.

Moreover, our view was that our focus on Colin's competence, using his own agenda, provided opportunities for him to begin to think about himself differently. He began to see the possibility of behaving differently as a real possibility. This in itself is the beginning of a different attitude. As he began behaving differently at school, and if parents and school personnel began to respond to this, not only would his new behaviour be likely to be reinforced, but also his emerging new view of himself. Thus, his behaviour is likely to generalise, and my expectation would be that, after a time, it would cease to be simply a means to an end. (Although, ultimately, if he were to continue to behave well, do better in his school work, and eventually gain his HSC, all just so that he could stay on the football team, who is to say that this would not be useful?).

6

The IMBALANCE
of RESPONSIBILITY

Typical patterns between students and adults

Many issues of conflict between parents and children, and between teachers and students, relate to the issue of responsibility. As mature and experienced adults, we want our children or students to show mature and responsible behaviour. Adults often find themselves in the position of taking more and more responsibility for encouraging children and adolescents to take more responsibility in their lives.

I once saw an adolescent with his parents, who sought my help with long-standing difficulties regarding his uncooperative, oppositional, and sometimes illegal antics. The parents were obviously extremely frustrated, desperate that their son should "wake up to himself" and 'realise that he needs to start taking some responsibility for his behaviour". They had been working extremely hard to try to convince him to take more responsibility.

At one point, his father said, "We have to keep on his back all the time — otherwise he doesn't do *anything*. You wouldn't believe how much we have to keep an eye on even the most basic things he should do.

The teenager interjected, "On my back? You wouldn't believe it. Nag, nag, nag, nag, nag ... they never let up. They keep on all the time."

"Well", said father, "if we didn't keep onto you, you wouldn't do a thing. I mean … (turning to me) … would you believe … he didn't even brush his teeth last night?"

Quietly, and sullenly, the young man said, "Well, you didn't tell me to brush my teeth last night."

I joked with the parents about whether, when their son reached 35 or 40, they might be phoning him every night to remind him to brush his teeth. I went on to suggest that it was understandable that they were concerned about his teeth. If they were to stop reminding him, I could not guarantee that his teeth would not fall out. However, if they were to continue to remind him, I could guarantee that he would *never* learn to remind himself.

This is a classic example of the imbalance of responsibility that often seems to characterise problems with children and, particularly, adolescents. I did not view these parents as unreasonable, or "overinvolved" — as some family therapy approaches would, with their ideas of "enmeshment" or of "overinvolved parents", or ideas that the parents were somehow benefitting from their son's problems (by forcing them to talk together, for example) — rather, it was clear that they were genuinely concerned for their son's well-being (and for their own dentist's bills!). However, they had become caught in a pattern whereby they were taking more and more responsibility for their son's behaviour, and he seemed to be taking less and less responsibility for his own behaviour.

Thinking in terms of interactional patterns, it seems that the more these parents strove to encourage their son to display more responsible behaviour, the more he seemed to embrace irresponsible behaviour. Whatever their motivation, and however well-meaning their intentions, the pattern had become entrenched such that they were "doing" all the work of responsibility and leaving little room for their son to display any real responsibility.

Cade (1989) poses the question, "Why would you buy a dog and bark yourself?". He comments,

If one person begins to become over-responsible, it is as though they begin to gather up more than their share of the total responsibility available in the relationship so that the other takes less responsibility, or counters with an opposite such as incompetence or irresponsibility. If you buy a dog and then continue to bark whenever someone knocks on the door, why would the dog do anything more than sleep and eat biscuits? Yet seeing the other's incompetence or irresponsibility becomes the understandable reason for taking on more of the responsibility, and then more of the same leads to more of the same, and so on, and a polarization can happen and become entrenched very quickly.

As the too-responsible person works harder and harder, the other, perhaps experiencing increasing levels of anger, disqualification and guilt, is likely to become increasingly more incompetent or irresponsible thus leaving that person with an accordingly increasing amount of responsibility. (Cade, 1989, p. 115).

It is a problem of being adult that we have learned the lessons of experience and we want the children and adolescents with whom we deal to have the same degree of responsibility and the same realisation of the consequences of not taking responsibility for their own behaviour..

Thus, when considering difficulties between children and adults, we should be alert for this kind of pattern. It is a particular example of the problem-maintaining interactional patterns that we might look for when conducting our "assessment" of a situation and, whilst only one of many different such patterns, is one which we encounter with great frequency.

Such responsibility patterns may be manifest in escalating conflict between adolescent and adults, as the adults work harder and harder to encourage greater responsibility and become increasingly frustrated as the adolescent seems to show less and less. Alternatively, they may be evident when an adolescent seems to continue with "irresponsible" behaviour that is inadvertently supported by adults "protecting" him or her from the consequences of that behaviour.

A colleague told me about a meeting she had with the staff of a particular school, when she had talked with them about the patterns of "responsibility — irresponsibility" that often seemed to occur. The teachers to whom she was speaking murmured their agreement. As she was speaking, there was a knock at the door. A student entered and said that he had forgotten his lunch. Various teachers made comments such as "What, again?". However, my colleague told me that at least six hands immediately went into their respective pockets and offered the money for lunch.

Again, the motivation here was well-intentioned. In many cases, where a student has forgotten his or her lunch, teachers lending the money to buy lunch would be a completely reasonable and helpful gesture. However, if the student has become a chronic lunch-forgetter, the confidence that "it will be okay ... they will give me some money to buy it" means that a change in behaviour is not really required. Even if the money is accompanied by lectures along the lines of "try to remember next time", the student has not had to face the consequences of his or her forgetting and so is no more likely to remember next time.

One of my son's teachers once commented how well he was progressing at reading but how often he seemed to be the one student who forgot to bring his reading book to school. Concerned that he would fall behind the rest of the class, she suggested that I might make a greater effort to ensure that he remembered his book each day. I commented that my nagging or reminding was unlikely to have any effect and that the only way I could ensure that he had his book would be to check his bag after he was asleep and then put the book in there myself. I was not sure that this would be helpful to him in the longer term and it ran the risk of establishing a pattern that we would regret later. I suggested that I ought *not* take over responsibility for him taking his book, but that she had my full support in imposing appropriate consequences for his forgetfulness.

It is understandable, but unfortunate, how often schools seem to ask parents to assume responsibility for their children's (mis)behaviour. All too often this has the effect of transferring the conflict from school to home but not really addressing the issue.

My experience is that children and adolescents, when adults stop assuming the responsibility for their behaviour, generally begin to behave differently.

A Year 10 girl once said to me, "Can't they see that, if they stopped nagging me about studying, I would probably do it?" Of course, "probably" was the important word here. Given the escalating pattern that had developed, I thought it likely that she *would* study more if her parents stopped pushing her to do so, but I could not guarantee it. However, I was fairly certain that I *could* guarantee that she would continue *not* studying if they continued pushing.

7 INTEVENING in PROBELM BAHVIOURS

REFRAMING

Reframing is fundamental to the brief therapy approaches. Once we "see" things in a particular way, we tend to continue to see them in that way, and our behaviour will be determined by that way of seeing. Reframing offers a different way of seeing the situation which may open the possibility of different responses.

> We would propose reframing to be the most basic and necessary operation in the process of change. Everything else is subordinate and either aids or, alternatively, impedes this process, or can be seen as the trimmings that reflect any particular therapist's beliefs and prejudices about therapy and the nature of change (not necessarily unhelpful in their therapy but sometimes unhelpful in the development of theoretical clarity). (Cade & O'Hanlon, 1993, pp. 113–114)

de Shazer (1991) offers a graphic example in his account of therapy with a couple, where the problem with which the woman presented was that she had become a nymphomaniac, needing to have sexual intercourse at least every night before going to sleep. The therapist's attempts to focus on exceptions to the problem became stuck when the woman was unable to see them as different. She had been able to force herself not to have sex on a couple of nights, however she did not see forcing herself not to satisfy this

INTERVENTIONS TO BRING ABOUT CHANGE

Reframing (altering how the problem is viewed)
- for the student — a new view of the situation may lead to different behaviour
- for the teacher — a new view of the situation may lead to different responses

Pattern interruption (altering the "doing" of the problem)
- introduce a (small) change into the habitual sequence of events that surrounds the problem
- small changes lead to bigger changes
- a deliberate small change brings an otherwise "unconscious" habit into conscious control

Observational tasks
- Look out for those times that you are successful/that things go well/that you do something different
- Yields information about success that can be built on and orients the client towards success

Practising (or continuing) success
- Do more of what works — building on exceptions or pre-session change
- Practising small steps that are part of the solution picture

Pretend tasks
- Act "as if" the miracle/solution/goal has been achieved
- Allows clients to behave differently, others to look for difference, and adds an element of fun.

Do something different
- Introduce an element of unpredictability
- When all else fails, do something different.

overpowering urge as at all positive — since it was the urge itself that was the problem. As the therapist explored the couple's despair, the husband talked of the tiredness that this problem was producing, since he wife could not go to sleep without having sex. In the process of the discussion, the problem was reframed as being one of "insomnia". This description did not carry the same overtones of serious pathology and allowed therapist and clients to move forward, and therapy focused on ways of getting to sleep rather than ways of not having sex.

Kral (1986) gives the example of a teacher reframing a student's disruptive, talking behaviour as a signal that the teacher is moving too quickly for the class to follow, thus attributing a more helpful (if misguided) intention to the behaviour; and of a counsellor suggesting to a teacher that a particular student's passive, non-participatory behaviour is thoughtfulness rather than resistance, with the result that the teacher is likely to be more patient.

As mentioned earlier, Molnar and Lindquist (1989, p. 48) give the example of a group of boys who entered the classroom noisily each morning and proceeded to talk loudly across the room, comparing their views of the previous evening's television shows, without doing their work. The teacher might "frame" this as deliberately disruptive behaviour, or as work-avoidance, leading to more and more attempts to take control — and, probably, to an escalating "battle". However, the teacher was able to reframe the behaviour (initially, just to herself) in a way that gave it a more benign connotation. When she thought of it as the boys being good friends and needing to affirm their friendship by "catching up" with each other, the situation no longer needed to be a power struggle. When she used this new explanation in responding to the boys, their behaviour no longer meant the same thing and gradually subsided.

Of course, it should be stressed again that we are here considering situations that have become "stuck". This is not to imply that teachers should not seek to take control of difficult behaviour on occasions. However, once an impasse is reached, a different perspective is required.

Cade (1990) gives an example of the way in which the label "hyperactive" was restricting, providing no possibility of feeling able to deal with the behaviour. When he framed the child as "extremely energetic", the possibility of channelling that energy became available.

Examples of reframing	
disruptive, uncooperative	awkward, unconfident
non-participatory, passive	thoughtful, careful
lazy	unhurried, "laid back"
demanding, critical teacher	believes students are capable of high standards
uninvolved parents, don't care	parents who trust the school's expertise

Some may argue that reframing along these lines is simplistic — "everybody KNOWS that he is lazy, so calling it careful and laid back just will not work!" Of course, as with any intervention, it must FIT the situation well enough to be acceptable. However, since there are potentially many "truths" about a situation or behaviour, a reframe can often make a difference even if people are at first sceptical about it.

In fact, teachers have been reframing behaviour for years, at least implicitly. Many a teacher knows that a consistently disruptive student will often respond well to being given some "special" job or responsibility. In a sense, this is implicitly reframing the behaviour as "eager to be involved" or "not enough to do" rather than responding to it as if it were deliberate misbehaviour.

Molnar and Lindquist (1989) include many examples where a teacher simply decided to reframe a student's behaviour in his or her own mind. More often, a teacher or counsellor will reframe the behaviour to the student, perhaps as an explanation for responding differently to it ("I realize how important it is to you to be able to answer questions in class, so I have decided to have five special questions for you in each lesson")

PATTERN INTERRUPTION

As mentioned, an important aspect of the MRI way of thinking about problems is the notion that problems are maintained through patterns of behaviour or interaction. We all lead patterned lives — that is, many of the things we do happen in the same ways and with the same sequences of actions. Thus, behaviours become familiar and "automatic" to us. Without these patterns, our lives would be chaotic; patterns provide stability and regularity and are not, in themselves, a problem. Problems, however, persist because they become part of patterns which get stuck.

> For the benefit of stability, they pay the price of rigidity, living, as all human beings must, in an enormously complex network of mutually supporting presuppositions ... change will require various sorts of relaxation or contradiction within the system of presuppositions. (Bateson, 1980, pp.158-159)

That is, the patterns surrounding behaviour are related to the beliefs or presuppositions we use to make sense of our experience. We may introduce a "relaxation or contradiction" within the network by altering how the problem is viewed (as in reframing) *or* by altering the pattern or sequence itself — since interrupting the pattern necessarily leads to a change in the way things are viewed.

Erickson would "devise an intervention that would alter some aspect of the symptom complex. ... Once the ... client [alters] one aspect of the symptom, he may be able to alter other aspects of the symptom. This could ultimately result in resolution of the presenting problem" (O'Hanlon, 1987, p. 33).

Pattern intervention may address the individual's problem pattern (a person who always smokes whilst watching TV might be told that, if she wishes to smoke, she must do so only whilst walking the dog) or the interactional pattern (a teacher who *always* responds a particular student's smart" remarks by telling her not to be so rude, which results in another remark, followed by another lecture about manners, etc., might be advised to compliment the student on his sense of humour).

The essential aspect of pattern intervention is finding out what sequence of behaviour *typically* surrounds the problem behaviour and then altering it or adding to it.

O'Hanlon recounts a case of Erickson's where he saw a boy who habitually sucked his thumb. When Erickson discovered that the boy always sucked his left thumb, he instructed him to give "equal time" to his right thumb ... and, later, to his other fingers (O'Hanlon, 1987, p. 38). This is a good example of how pattern intervention may be employed with behaviours that seem "habitual" — since the altering of the pattern makes the behaviour now something under conscious control.

Molnar and Lindquist (1989, p. 102) give an example of a student who blurted out answers in class, behaviour seen by the teacher as "attention seeking", thus the teacher responds by ignoring the behaviour, leading to the student blurting even more. They suggest that the teacher could interrupt the typical pattern by telling the student that he must move to a particular desk in the room (the "blurt desk") before blurting out answers, or that he must write down his blurt first, before blurting vocally.

I saw an interview in which Steve de Shazer made a small alteration in the pattern of nagging/ haranguing by a mother and ignoring by her child. He asked the mother to write her "nags" on paper and give them to her son silently. Had he simply asked her to "back off", she may have objected that it was important that she correct her son, since he needed to learn correct behaviour. de Shazer's task meant that she was still able to "get her message across" but the pattern of confrontation was interrupted.

Molnar and Lindquist (1989, p. 106) give another example involving a persistent impasse between teacher and student, because the student seemingly "refused" do do any mental arithmetic but wrote even the simplest problems down on scraps of paper. Instead of continuing to encourage her to solve problems mentally, the teacher finally reframed the situation as "the student being concerned that she got everything right" and asked her to use a special book, to make sure that she wrote down *every* aspect of *every* problem, and that she showed her book to another teacher to be checked. Thus, the pattern was changed by changing scrap paper to a special book, and writing down surreptitiously to writing down and having checked. The student eventually decided that doing the calculations in her head was quicker.

Of course, in each of these examples, the pattern intervention entailed a direct request to do something in a different way. Thus, they relied on the counsellor achieving rapport and cooperation such that the client was a "customer". Whether we suggest to teachers that they interrupt a pattern, or suggest it to students or parents, our suggestion must make sense, which entails having the right agenda, establishing rapport, and perhaps reframing the situations.

OBSERVATIONAL TASKS (Notice something different)

de Shazer and Molnar (1984) outlined what they termed "four useful interventions in brief family therapy". The first of these was so useful it became known as the "formula first session task" — that is, it proved a useful task to give at the end of a first counselling session, almost regardless of the nature of the client(s).

> *Between now and the next time we meet, we want you to observe, so that you can tell us next time, what happens in your family that you want to continue to have happen (1984, p. 298)*

de Shazer (1988) describes this as one of the "skeleton keys" to the lock on the door of change, since the task is useful without a detailed assessment of the problem — or even if it is not clear exactly what the problem is. Rather, this task assumes that it can be helpful in therapy to identify whatever is going *right*, and then seek to build on this.

Exceptions are powerful foundations of change. This task is a request to look for exceptions. People come to therapy often preoccupied with how bad things are, and this preoccupation colours their view of everything. A task that asks them to focus on what is going well helps reorient their view of the situation, and provides the counsellor with positive steps to discuss in the next session.

In a case with a girl struggling with an "obsessive-compulsive" problem, my intervention at the end of the first session, having reframed the situation as "fears pushing you around", was:

> What I'd suggest is that every night, or every couple of days, you sit down with Mum or with Dad or with Mum and Dad, and ask yourself "Have there been any times today when I've not done what the fears wanted me to do?" "Are there any times today when I've pushed them around — even just a bit." You might be able to think of some, and then maybe Mum and Dad might be able to think of some that you didn't even real-

ise. 'Cos we know that these fears don't even like you thinking about the times you boss them around. I guess they worry that you might feel too strong. So you might think about any times when you didn't give in to them completely, you didn't let them have their way with you completely. (Durrant, 1989, p. 22)

Both parents and child had been overwhelmed by the seeming pervasiveness of the problem. However, nothing happens 100% of the time, and my assumption was that there would be lots of times when, even in small ways, this girl managed things differently. This intervention was an attempt to "orient" the family to look out for these times since, if they could recognise them, that would affect their view of the situation and so their outlook on success.

Whilst writing this book, I saw a family where parents and adolescent (Year 10) were in continued conflict issues as homework. Not surprisingly, my exploration of the situation revealed that this conflict was repeated over many other issues — tidying her room, paying attention to her parents' views, spending time with her younger siblings, and so on. My sense was that her parents wanted me somehow to "fix her". Perhaps they thought that I could "talk sense into her", where they had failed. Certainly, my view was that they were unlikely to respond well to a direct suggestion that they do something differently.

After ensuring that I had responded to their frustration and their concern for their daughter's future, I ended the session by asking that they be on the lookout, over the ensuing week, for any sign, no matter small, that she was capable of behaving more responsibly. I explained that I found counselling proceeded more quickly if we were able to find some things to "build on", rather than having to start from scratch in developing new behaviours, thus the information they would find would be important in giving us a direction. They seemed satisfied with this explanation and were happy to carry out the task.

A week or so later, the family returned and the parents seemed a little less frantic about the situation than they had been at our first meeting. They had "discovered" a number of occasions on which their daughter had done some household task without having to be asked and reminded. When I asked them how they accounted for this, they were unsure — maybe she had begun to change. I explored these incidents, and the differences they had made, and it seemed that her parents had actually "backed off" a bit from their persistent nagging. My detailed exploration of all the differences they had noticed was designed to help these become more "real". That is, they entered with a list of particular events and my aim was to help them begin to view their daughter differently on the basis of these.

Observational tasks of this type can be very useful and lead to surprising changes. They can be given to individuals to observe themselves, or to observe the other party to the interaction, and can be tailored to fit the particular situation.

- Observe what happens when you keep your temper under control
- Keep a look out for any things that you do which are in the direction you want things to go.
- See if you can catch the teacher out when she's not on your back, and note down what you are doing different at those times.
- Look out for any times that she seems even a little more cooperative.
- Take note, so you can tell me next time, what you do when you overcome the urge to hit somebody

Of course, these questions include the suggestion that these successes *will* happen and so help orient the person towards success.

PRACTISING (or CONTINUING) SUCCESS

One of the key principles of brief therapy is "if it works, keep doing it". It is surprising how often, once a counselling session has elicited details of exceptions and already-existing successes, and has explored how the client has been able to make these happen, intervention is then simply a matter of encouraging him or her to keep doing it.

As de Shazer suggests, "now you know what works, do more of it" (1988, p. xiii)

A student came to talk with me about his difficulties with peer relations. He was the focus of a great deal of teasing and abuse and found this interfering with his schoolwork. It also led to his frequently losing his temper, with the result that he was the one who spent the rest of lunchtime at the Principal's office. I asked him about "the last time when you felt you handled things better" and he was able to tell me about an incident in which he managed to ignore the remarks directed at him. As we explored this exception, he told me that his different response was motivated by desperation rather than being a strategy he had devised, however he "realised", as we talked, that the other students had given up on their teasing. He remembered that he had also taken the initiative in talking to one of the other students, at another time and about something unrelated to the teasing, and that this student had been relatively friendly. Again, he had not really been aware of this at the time — he needed to find out about some homework and this student was the only person from his class around at the time. However, in our conversation, he saw that his taking the initiative in this way had led to a different kind of interaction with the other student.

My suggestion to him was that he might continue to work on ignoring the remarks, since he had discovered for himself that this worked. Moreover, perhaps he should make a deliberate effort to speak to *one* of the other students each day. This did not need to be a lengthy conversation; it might be little more than asking the time — what was important was that he take the initiative.

When he returned, he told me that he had not needed to work on ignoring the teasing, because it had "magically" stopped. He had begun to get on much better with the four or five students who had been his main abusers (although he was satisfied that they might never be good friends) and felt much more confident about school. I am unsure whether his initiating conversations interrupted the pattern and solved the problem, whether he did, in fact, ignore the teasing but was so successful that he did not notice it, or whether his feeling that he had some strategies gave him sufficient confidence that he no longer invited teasing.

It seems all too simple — but the problem with our training is that it often leads us to ignore what is simple. What was important was that the strategies he decided to use arose from the discussion of what he had already done. Had I simply given him advice about strategies to try, he might not have been as confident.

One of the simple, but surprising, discoveries is that clients have often already begun to solve their problems. Weiner-Davis et al (1987) routinely asked clients about what changes they had noticed between making the request or appointment for counselling and attending the session. In 67% of cases, clients were able to report that things had been better to some degree — although they tended not to talk about these changes unless asked. Students might be asked what they have noticed that has been different since making the appointment to see the counsellor, or teachers might be asked what has been different since they first requested the counsellor's help. Any such changes should not be dismissed as aberrations or chance events, but explored and built upon. They become significant if we make them significant.

Abigail, 15 and in Year 10, was referred after continued altercations with teachers leading to the threat of suspension. Her mother described her ongoing frustration at Abigail's failure to "come to her senses", commenting that her daughter was very intelligent and independent (qualities which "helped" her get into trouble) and should be able to figure out how to do better.

After getting only a brief description of the nature of the problem, I asked what had been better in the couple of weeks since they had made the appointment to see me. Abigail said, "Not much", although she thought that maybe she had not been in as much trouble. I wondered how this had happened and if she thought she had been doing something differently, and she thought that she had been "trying" harder. As I explored, in detail, what "trying harder" had entailed, and how she had been able to do it, Mum told me that there had been a major incident at school the previous week, when Abigail had been caught skipping classes. My fear was that Mum was about to redirect the focus of the interview to the problem and I was taken off guard when she added, "and I was quite proud of how she handled it."

Apparently, Abigail had not lost her temper when being spoken to by the Principal and had negotiated with him about changing the time of the detention which he imposed. Mother was clear that the truanting had upset her but, nonetheless, she saw the way Abigail had dealt with the situation as a change. Encouraged by this, I continued to ask about what had been different. Mother had noticed Abigail's "trying harder", particularly since Abigail was coming home and talking to her about what had happened at school rather than keeping it to herself. Both agreed that this had meant that there was considerably less tension at home.

I expressed how impressed I was by the changes that Abigail had been able to make. Her explanation was that the threatened suspension had made her "come to my senses". We spent some time detailing specific behaviours that were part other acting more sensibly. I asked both, on a scale of 0 to 10, how confident they were that Abigail could keep up these changes. Abigail's confidence was "7 or 8", whilst mother's confidence was "9". She said that she knew Abigail could manage it, as long as she wanted to do so.

We finished with my conceding that I could offer no advice that was any better than the advice Abigail had given herself, and encouraged her to continue doing what was (now) working.

Parents and teachers often hope that a dire threat will shock a student and bring the student "to his or her senses". However, in itself, the threat of suspension may simply entrench the situation. What was important in this case was to focus on what had already changed and build a detailed description of it.

If exceptions are not as obvious or accessible, or the suggestion to do more of what has worked does not seem to fit, I have found the idea of "practising" new behaviour to be helpful. I have described an approach to working with children and adolescents in residential units which seeks to frame the entire residential period as a time of practice (Durrant, 1993). The idea of practice includes the notion that it does not have to work *all* the time — the desired change can be broken into small steps and these practised one at a time. Children readily relate to analogies about practising a musical instrument or practising a sporting activity.

Future-focused questions, such as the miracle question and scaling questions, yield information about goals. I have suggested that we should explore these answers in detail, painting a detailed picture of what the client will *be doing* when the goal is reached. It is then possible to ask the client to choose one of the (small) new behaviours and practice that in the next week or so.

• Okay, so you've told me a number of things that you will be doing differently when you move from 4 to 5 on that growing up scale. How about you pick one of those things that you will be doing when you get to 5 and practice it over the next week?

In discussing how the answers to the miracle question were used to establish manageable goals with a client, some colleagues explained,

The miracle question led to a number of specific behaviors — spending more time with her sister, looking for a job [etc.] ... It was then possible to discuss ways that she might deliberately practice some of these. These activities became steps towards her goal, and each might then be explored to identify the intermediate steps she could practice. So, for example, talking about possible jobs, looking in the newspaper, practicing writing job applications, perhaps role-playing job interviews, and so on, are all activities that might be undertaken. Because these are derived from the elaboration of [the client's] goal, they become meaningful activities rather than just things imposed by staff as being "things you should do". (Durrant, 1993, p. 68)

These specific behaviours to be practised might not always immediately seem apparent from an identification of the problem. In the example above, the "presenting problem" concerned depression and hearing voices. Writing job applications is not a logically obvious way to treat these psychiatric problems. However, looking for a job *was* one of the things that was identified as what *will be happening* were the miracle to occur. Thus, it was a meaningful thing to practice as part of constructing the solution.

With children and adolescents with so-called "behaviour problems", it is often easy for teachers to construct a list of what the student "needs to do differently". If we then suggest that the student practice some of these new behaviours, it may easily seem like a a different way of simply asking for compliance. However, specific behaviours or changes that the student identifies as part of the description of the miracle, or in answer to "How will you know when you are ready to return to that class?" are more likely to lead to meaningful steps that might be practiced.

PRETEND TASKS (act "AS IF")

Milton Erickson said, "You can pretend anything and achieve it" (Lustig, 1975).

de Shazer (1991) describes a therapy case with clients who had significant psychiatric diagnoses and histories, in which he asked each of them to choose two days during the following week, unknown to the other, and to pretend that the miracle had happened. They were each to try to pick the two days that the other chose to pretend.

Having built a description of the things that will be happening when the solution is achieved, one possibility is to ask the person concerned to "pretend" that it has occurred. It is surprising that people who seem unwilling or unable to practice the steps identified as being part of the desired solution will often be quite happy to engage in a pretend task.

In the example from de Shazer, the task has a number of aspects. First, asking each of the clients to *pretend* that the miracle has happened is much less daunting than asking them to *try* to be different. Pretending involves doing all or some of the new behaviours, however there is less pressure to be compliant. Second, the "pick two days, secretly, to pretend" introduced an element of fun into the task. Third, the request to try to pick which two days the other chose meant that each was "on the lookout" for different behaviour. Even if one or both did not carry out the pretending, the task was still likely to be successful since it is likely that each would notice some differences in the other anyway.

A teacher was prepared to "try anything I suggested" with a Year 6 boy who was constantly disruptive in the classroom. I interviewed the boy and the teacher together and asked both the miracle question. The teacher's description of the miracle was largely a list of more compliant behaviour that she would see from the boy, however I persisted to explore how these behaviours would make a difference and she suggested things such as "he will seem happier". "How will you know that he seems happier?", I asked, and she mentioned things such as his putting up his hand to answer questions, choosing a reading book that he enjoyed, and colouring in his work in his book. The boy, initially, was fairly sullen but was gradually able to describe how things would be different after the miracle. He mentioned such things as being able to make a joke without getting yelled at (and the teacher commented that he *did* have a good sense of humour but that she often feared that laughing at his jokes would just encourage him to talk more) and feeling that the teacher would say something nice about his work.

After commenting that the continued confrontation seemed "a drag" for both of them, I suggested that the student choose two "sessions" in class (that is, before recess, between recess and lunch, or after lunch) over the next few days, and pretend that the miracle had occurred. That is, he was to pretend that she did not feel like throwing things at other students, was having fun, and was enjoying his work. I stressed that this was only pretend — he did not *really* have to enjoy his work — and he assured me that he thought he could manage this. The teacher was to try to guess which sessions the student chose as his"pretend times" but she was not to make any comment.

Again, the student did not really have to try to be different, he just had to *pretend* to be different,. This introduces an important "saving face" element into any changes that happen. The fact that the miracle times were secret introduced the element of trying to "trick" the teacher — something most students are more than happy to do. Of course, even if the student did not pretend, the teacher was looking for different behaviour and so was more likely to respond to any examples, however small, of his behaving differently.

In this case, I did not ask the teacher to pretend, although I could have done. However, the very fact of the detailed exploration of the miracle probably led to the teacher doing some things differently anyway.

I recently worked with a 20-year-old young man, Gavin, with a mild intellectual disability, whose parents were concerned that he was "preoccupied with sex". Given his disability, they were realistic in conceding that they did not know what opportunities he might have for forming relationships and expressing his sexuality, however they were concerned about his masturbating in public, watching pornographic videos in the presence of their younger children, and so on. I spent a couple of sessions with Gavin (slowly and repetitively, given his level of understanding and concentration) identifying exceptions — times he had shown self-control. This was helpful to a point.

In our third session, I said that his Mum had said she was worried he was preoccupied with sex. Gavin asked what this meant and, when I said it meant "you think about sex all the time", he readily agreed, grinning widely. I was concerned that I should not try to "convince" him that he had a problem, however I was aware that this was something which could lead to difficulties for him. I suggested it meant that "sex is in charge of your thinking". As we discussed this, he agreed that it might be better to think about sex when *he* wanted to, rather than sex "controlling his brain".

I asked the miracle question and, initially, Gavin was only able to answer that the miracle would be that "sex would not be in charge of my thinking". I persisted with asking what would be different?, how that would make a difference?, what would his parents notice?, how would they respond differently?, and so on. Gradually, he said things like, "The kids (his siblings) won't be scared of me ... and I'll be playing with them more", "Mum might like me ... I'll talk to her more about what I've been doing", and so on. Specific differences were things like, "I will rent different videos from the video shop —

like 'Three men and a baby' instead of the R-rated ones I usually get".

I suggested that, each night, he should toss a coin. If the coin came up "heads", then the next day he was to pretend that the miracle had happened. If it came up "tails", he should do whatever he normally did. He seemed to think that this would be fun.

When Gavin returned a week or so later, he told me that, the first night the coin had come up "heads". Before I had a chance to ask about this, he said, "and the second night was heads, and the third night ... heads". I began to be concerned that I had inadvertently placed him under too much pressure and perhaps should have used a "pick two days to pretend" task instead. "And the fourth night, it was tails". I immediately feared that one "tails" day had probably plunged him back into the problem. "But, I made it heads instead!".

"Then the fifth night, I didn't toss the coin at all". My worst fears were confirmed — I was sure he had probably given the task away. However, to my surprise, he added, "Because it happened." I wondered what had happened. "You know, that miracle, it happened".

Later, when his father came to collect him, I invited him in and Gavin told him, "It happened, Dad ... the miracle happened". Father seemed bemused but, as I asked him what he had noticed, he commented, "yes, you know, something was different last week. We couldn't quite figure out what it was, but things were ... well ... less pressured".

Berg and Miller (1992) comment that the "coin toss" task is a useful way to help clients get unstuck, introducing an element of unpredictability into the pretend task, but comment that it is most useful for clients who have some commitment to the particular goals — that is, who are "customers" (but, remember that a client who is not a "customer" may be so if the problem and/or the goals are defined differently).

Many clients who are willing to take steps are intrigued by this suggestion. They are curious about what will turn up at the toss of the coin, and they look forward to finding out what their "luck" will be. Some clients even enjoy what appears to be a childlike game and get into the spirit of the suggestion, because they realize that their previous serious attempts at solutions did not work. (Berg & Miller, 1992, p. 123)

Pretend tasks can be used with students and teachers, with students alone, and with students and parents. I have often used the miracle question when working with parents and adolescents with longstanding conflict and responsibility imbalance, and have used the "pick two days to pretend that the miracle has happened" task with both adolescent and parent. In nearly every case, they have returned reporting that things have been better.

As with the previous discussion of imagining the solution, through the miracle, or steps towards the solution, through scaling questions, it is equally possible to use pretend tasks where the student is asked to "pretend that you have reached 6 on the scale".

DO SOMETHING DIFFERENT

An important principle of brief therapy is "if it works, keep doing it". The converse is equally important — "if it is not working, do something different".

I have sometimes commented to clients, after seeking to validate their experience of hopelessness and impasse, that I'm not sure what they can do about their situation, however I agree with them that what they are doing now is not working. I suggest that, when what you are doing is not working, it is important to do something different. "It almost doesn't matter what it is — as long as it is different!" Doing something different is a variation on pattern interruption. Certainly, if a teacher, a student, or a parent does something different when the problem occurs, this has the effect of interrupting the pattern that exists around the problem. Doing something different often changes the meaning of habitual behaviours.

Doing something different can involve almost anything that changes what usually happens.

Ron was a boy of 13 years of age in Year Seven at school. He was identified by his teacher as being extremely immature and was beginning to fall behind in his academic work. Although during the course of the interview it became evident that there were some difficulties at home, they were not sufficiently serious to motivate the family to seek therapy. The main problem specified was an inability of the parents to communicate with Ron. ...

The crux of the difficulty according to the teacher was that Ron could not accept any negative feedback. When papers were returned in class, Ron would have a temper tantrum if he had even one error. The temper tantrum involved tearing up the returned work, stomping to the rubbish bin, throwing it out, and sulking. This behaviour was hard to ignore by the rest of the class and, consequently, Ron had very few friends.

Ron and his teacher were told that more information was required to aid in better understanding of the problem by everyone. One way of getting more understanding is by Ron pretending to have a temper tantrum and if there were no mistakes on the returned papers, for Ron's teacher to pretend that there were mistakes. It was argued that, during a tantrum, Ron was too involved to be objective enough to gain more understanding of the situation. Only while pretending can he be a keen observer of the reactions of others to his temper tantrums. It was agreed that the teacher should give Ron a secret signal when he had marked a question wrong which was actually correct. This way, both the teacher and Ron would know that it was only a pretend incorrect answer. Ron seemed very keen to participate in this task.

Two weeks later they were seen again to discuss the task. The teacher was pleased to report that there had been no temper tantrums, either real or pretend, during the intervening period in spite of a number of papers being returned. Ron simply had not completed the task. (Brown, 1986, p. 13).

In this example, the teacher and student were asked to do something that was quite different to their usual interaction. Pretending was used, however it was pretending to have the problem rather than pretending that the solution had occurred. In a sense, the task took the usual behaviours of both teacher and student and turned them into a game. Thus, they could not continue to mean the same as they had done before.

I have described earlier the characteristic pattern that often occurs with adolescents where adults are working harder and harder to "take responsibility" for the adolescent being more responsible, and the adolescent seeming to show less and less responsibility. This pattern needs turning on its head, however — at least in the minds of the adults — the stakes are high. When working with parents and adolescents stuck in this pattern, I often sympathise at length with the parents, validating their concerns about their son or daughter's future, and commiserate with them that what they are doing, whilst apparently sensible, is simply not working. I then suggest that they "do something different" next time the pattern shows itself.

Cade (1988) recounts a case example which he calls "Putting stepmother down".

> Sonia had recently married John — his second marriage, to which he had brought three teenagers. It was Sonia's first marriage, and she was determined quickly to earn the children's love and respect, and to avoid becoming the archetypal "wicked stepmother".

> Sonia was seriously considering whether she could stand the thought of returning home after the appointment, such was her level of stress. She experienced James (15) as taking every opportunity to belittle her, often in front of friends and particularly in front of John's business contacts. These "put-downs" were usually extremely subtle (though nonetheless hurtful, and apparent to all but the most insensitive observer) and, if faced, he would look puzzled or hurt, and claim to have been joking, or misinterpreted. John found himself powerless to help. For example, James constantly and superciliously belittled her for the television programmes she enjoyed, for the books she read. Sonia had never been to university. At a recent important dinner party, attended by a number of his father's literary business contacts, he had loudly and apparently innocently asked Sonia, "Mum, which university did you ... Oh no, you didn't get to university, did you?"

> He would rarely eat what she cooked, always finding fault and usually cooking his own meal, leaving the kitchen in a terrible mess, responding to her requests that he tidy up with "genuine" promises to

do it later which he never kept. Sonia usually ended up clearing his things away. He had clapped and cheered loudly as she left for work that morning, which had hurt her profoundly. As John, who seemed extremely concerned about his wife's level of distress, commented, "He is so clever that, when faced with any of these things, he always looks taken aback, saying, 'I'm sorry, I don't know what you mean', claiming that he had not intentionally done anything to hurt".

Sonia felt embarrassed talking of these things since each example seemed so trite. She said that it was like water torture. One drip onto the forehead was of little consequence; it was the endless, unrelenting succession of drips that eventually drove a person mad. In attempting to deal with this problem, Sonia had been alternately appealing to James, asking him why he was doing it to her, berating him, explaining how hurtful it was, demanding of him what he wanted from her, trying to reason, demanding that John speak to him. Nothing seemed to have made any difference. He could still, almost without effort, "pull the strings" that rendered her helpless and desperate.

It was clear they were seriously neglecting both their marriage and themselves, and their concerns about James filled most of their time. They agreed, but Sonia said that, unless she could find an answer to this difficulty with James, she could not see them even beginning to address these areas. None of the children knew they were seeking professional help. I asked if they would be prepared to try an experiment for a week or so, although it would probably be more demanding on her than him. They were willing to try anything, particularly once they had accepted that everything they had tried so far seemed to have had no effect, or even had exacerbated the problem.

I advised Sonia that, although I understood how the many things James said or did were often like a knife plunged into her stomach, from now on I wanted her to experiment with (1) completely ignoring them, or (2) putting herself down slightly more than he had. The former was to be done "quietly rather than noisily" (i.e., just to ignore him rather than give a pained and strained non-verbal message "look how I am ignoring you" such that it would still be clear that the behaviour or comment was having an effect). If he made a derisory comment on a television programme she was watching or book she was reading, she was to comment that it was the only level of programme or book she could cope with, others being too hard for her to understand. This reply was to be made without the slightest hint of anger or sarcasm, in a purely matter-of-fact voice, though she was not to go out of her way to make such comments. If he made a comment about university, she was to point out, again in a matter-of-fact way, that she had been too stupid to go to university. If he was again to clap and cheer as she left for work, she was either to ignore it, bow and wave (though not to go back to make a point of doing it), or to comment with gentle humour that it must be a relief that, now she was leaving, the average level of intelligence in the house would go up, only to come down again once she returned home. At no point was she, under any circumstance, to discuss or reason with him, or express anger at, the put-downs.

From now on, if James made a mess in the kitchen, she was only once to ask him politely to tidy it up. If he ignored her, she was not to mention it again, nor tidy it up herself. When John returned home, he was automatically to tidy the kitchen, but without making an issue of it. He was not to draw his son's attention to the fact that it was **his** mess ... just do the tidying up (but make sure, if possible, that he did it at a time that James would be aware that he was doing it). If James asked why he was doing it, he was to reply that he'd just decided he would tidy up the kitchen before settling down for the evening (with no hint that he was doing a job that James **should** have done). If James, by any chance, asked why they were suddenly acting differently, they were to look puzzled and say they didn't know what he meant; they didn't realize they were acting differently.

As the couple left my office, Sonia had a mischievous grin on her face. "Do you know", she said, "I'm almost hoping he gives me a hard time tonight".

When they returned, three weeks later, Sonia expressed both delight and disappointment. She was delighted because the problem seemed no longer to exist. James had done nothing at all to put her down since the initial appointment. She was disappointed because she'd had no opportunity to try my suggestion. (Three year follow-up) James, though he is probably the most difficult of the three to cope with, has rarely attempted to put Sonia down in the way that he had relentlessly been doing when they came to see me. The children still do not know that their parents consulted me.

(Cade, 1988, pp. 28–30 — slightly edited)

This is a good example of getting people to "do something different". Had the therapist simply asked this woman to ignore her step-son's behaviour, she would probably have found numerous reasons not to do so. He spent quite some time developing the theme of "this is *awful* — and what is even more awful is that all your reasonable and understandable responses *simply are not working.*" Within this context, the woman was prepared to try something different.

This example also shows how the "something different" can often be framed as "an experiment". The counsellor is not promising that this will work, but simply offering it as an experiment. People seem more likely to comply with such experiments.

Similarly, I have often asked parents to "back off" from nagging their adolescent as a time-limited experiment, which will give us further information. They have been prepared to agree to this, where they would not have agreed to a suggestion that they "back off" if it was framed as THE solution to the problem.

David Epston, a New Zealand therapist, has described a graphic example of getting students and teacher to do something different (This example is unpublished and is written from my memory of David's description , with his permission).

Frank was a school student who was about to be suspended from school. He had a long history of playground fights, which had not responded to a variety of interventions. Family therapy, with frank and his parents, had similarly been unsuccessful. David elicited the school Principal's agreement to "try something different", and gave the Principal detailed instructions about what he should do.

The Principal called Frank into his office, along with the six boys with whom he most often fought. He explained to the boys that Frank was very close to being expelled from school, that the efforts of the school, Frank's parents, and a number of therapists had been unsuccessful in resolving this problem. Frank's only chance laid with these six boys.

"Now", he said, "I know that you re all very good at getting Frank to lose his cool — experts at it, from what I hear. Tell me, what are some of the names you can call Frank that get him really upset?"

The boys were understandably hesitant, however the Principal continued, "Joe, I hear that 'deadshit' is one of the names you can call Frank that get him upset. Is that right?" Joe grudgingly agreed, and the Principal continued to elicit a list of names that got Frank upset.

Finally, the Principal allocated one "name" to each student. "Joe, your word is 'deadshit'; Bill, your word is 'fuckwit'; Tony, your word is 'dork-head'," and so on. "Now, I want you to practice your words ... come on, it's okay ... you can do better than that."

"Now, and this is important, I want you to remember your word. Out in the playground, any time that you see Frank about to lose his cool, I want you to say your particular words to him — really let him have it. Remember, it is his only chance. And we will meet here every morning so you can practice."

My memory of the story is that Frank never had another playground fight again.

This is a powerful example of changing the meaning of the interaction by doing something (very) different. I suspect that many Principals would not be willing to try such a strategy, however.

CASE EXAMPLE —

8   Brief strategic intervention

The following case study is taken from a paper in which the author, a school psychologist, has used principles from a brief therapy approach to develop what he calls "Brief Strategic Family Intervention" (BSFI). The case demonstrates the use of the ideas when working with students directly and their families indirectly (that is, his work with the parents was only by phone).The case also shows how educational data-collecting techniques may be employed within the context of therapy intervention.

The paper is "Brief strategic family intervention for school-related problems", by John J Murphy (Family Therapy Case Studies, 1992, 7(1), 59–71) and this extract is reprinted with permission of the author.

Jill, a fourth grade girl in a gifted/talented school program, was referred to the school psychologist (the author) by her parents. The assessment/ intervention process occurred over a period of three weeks, involving four phone contacts with parents and two individual meetings with Jill.

Nature of the problem

Jill's parents were very concerned about her increased "anxiety" regarding school, citing that she performed the following behaviours on a daily

---

*   *John J Murphy is Director of Psychological Services, Covington Independent Schools District, 24 East 75th St., Covington, Kentucky 41011 USA.*

basis (excluding the weekend):

a) frequently asking to have her temperature taken;

b) pleading with parents to let her stay up later at night; and

c) pleading with her father to take her home upon being dropped off at school in the morning, sometimes refusing to leave the car.

Chief complainants

Of all the parties involved, the parents seemed to be the chief complainants who appeared most inconvenienced by the problem and, therefore, most motivated to solve it. Although Jill did not show the same urgency as her parents, she stated that she wanted "the whole thing to get better". School personnel had no concerns whatsoever about her behaviour or academic performance.

Positions regarding the problem

The parents generally viewed Jill as "troubled" and in need of support and encouragement. They considered themselves conscientious, involved parents. Although Jill was initially reluctant to meet with me because she didn't want anybody at school thinking she was crazy, she agreed to a "discussion" (as opposed to a "counselling session") with me in her home. She believed that her parents were "making too much" of the situation. When asked how she explained the problem, she said that her fears resulted from periodic criticisms from a "mean, unfair" teacher.

Previous solution attempts

The parents' primary approach to the problem was to point out to Jill the irrationality of her fears. As the problem worsened, the parents responded in kind by refining and strengthening their helping strategy (i.e. more of the same). When asked what she had done to cope with the teacher situation, Jill indicated that she tried "not to think about it", adding that the harder she tried, the more nervous she became. Thus, it appeared that the solution attempts on the part of Jill and her parents exacerbated the problem they were intending to resolve.

Minimal Goals

When I asked specifically how they would know when things were improving, Jill's parents stated that they would see a decrease in the number and severity of problem behaviours noted above. In addition to providing a concrete indicator of goal attainment for the parents, their observation of these behaviours was incorporated into the intervention task described below.

Interventions

In an attempt to interrupt the problem-engendering cycle discussed above, I suggested the following tasks.

Parents' Task

I sought to utilize the parents' desire to remain actively involved in helping their daughter by offering them the role of "observers and experimenters" in the intervention process. In addition to their daily recording of whether or not Jill asked to have her temperature taken, a subjective rating procedure was collaboratively developed whereby the parents were to rate the acceptability of Jill's morning and bedtime behaviour on a scale of 1 through 10 — where 1 represented "very unacceptable" and 10 "very acceptable".

I suggested to Jill's parents that, perhaps, they might actually be of more help and support to their daughter if they conveyed their confidence in her ability to resolve her own problems by "backing off", and they agreed to discontinue their usual lectures. They diligently maintained a cumulative record of daily ratings for more than two months. In an effort to empower them in their new approach, I complimented them periodically for the thoroughness of their record-keeping and their courage in holding to a strategy that, although apparently effective, was nonetheless difficult to implement at times.

Student's Task:

I asked Jill to record "mean marks" for every mean thing the teacher did during certain times of the day and explained that this would help me better understand the extreme "meanness" of the teacher. This task connected well with Jill's preoccupation with the teacher and her perception of the teacher's critical style. I told her that she need not do anything about the problem, but was simply to gather this information in order to help clarify the situation.

I also instructed Jill to not laugh during this data collection, since this could call more attention to her. This intervention disallowed Jill's previously unsuccessful attempts to avoid the teacher, as well as reframing her teacher observations from the previously apprehensive perspective to a different, more humorous context.

Jill readily accepted and implemented the task. She eagerly reported her data the following week, adding that she no longer felt nervous about the teacher or school. I told her that she had apparently "hit on something" that improved things, though it was unclear to me exactly what that "something" was. This statement was primarily intended to empower her with the rightful ownership of desired changes.

Results

Data from the daily parental observations suggested a marked decrease in the frequency and intensity of the presenting problems. Jill asked to have her temperature taken on each of the 10 baseline days, but on only the first two of 30 days following intervention.

The parents' daily ratings of Jill's morning and bedtime behaviours were averaged on a weekly basis, as presented in Figure 1. Compared to baseline ratings, Jill's parents rated her behaviour in both situations much more favourably during the seven weeks following intervention, and upon follow-up contacts.

Results of single-case studies, particularly those conducted in natural settings as part of one's routine job responsibilities, are typically subject to internal and external validity constraints. The results of this case study are certainly limited regarding their generalizability to other persons, problems, and circumstances (i.e., external validity). They are also subject to threats to internal validity (i.e., factors other than the reported interventions which may have contributed to desired changes). For example, "history" is one such threat that cannot feasibly by controlled because people experience many events which may influence targeted behaviours in addition to the intervention.

In order to strengthen inferences regarding intervention effects in this case study, certain data collection and analysis strategies were employed as recommended by Kazdin (1982) and Kratochwill (1985). First, adequate baseline data were gathered to assess the projected course of target behaviours. The inference of an intervention effect was enhanced by the favoura-

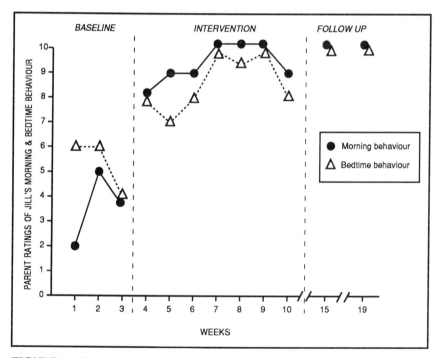

FIGURE 1. Parent ratings of the acceptability of Jill's morning and bedtime
behaviour (1 — "very unacceptable" ... 10 — "very acceptable")

ble, dramatic changes in all three target behaviours immediately following intervention. Second, score overlap was examined based on the notion that, the fewer the number of overlapping scores between baseline and intervention phases, the larger the intervention effect. As shown in Figure 1, there were no overlapping scores between baseline and intervention phases. Third, data were analysed by examining the variability and trend of scores between and within phases, based on Kazdin's (1982) point that highly variable intervention scores suggest greater caution in interpreting results. Although mean weekly parent ratings ranged from 8 to 10 for morning behaviour, and 7 to 10 for bedtime behaviour during the intervention phase, these ranges were comparable to the baseline ratings for both behaviours.

These strategies collectively strengthened inferences regarding the effectiveness of the intervention in promoting desired changes.

Discussion

This case highlights several important features of the brief strategic family intervention approach. The assessment and intervention focused only on the persons and interactions seen as directly and currently related to the maintenance of the problem. For example, school personnel were not included primarily because they did not express any complaints about Jill or her behaviour. Further, information was not gathered regarding Jill's early childhood development or experiences, intergenerational issues, personality type, and so on. This point is not intended as a blanket criticism of broader assessment and intervention approaches, but rather seeks to emphasize BSFI's present-future orientation and the specific goal of resolving presenting complaints.

Second, each person's problem definition and beliefs (that is, position) regarding the problem were accepted and incorporated into the rationale and content of interventions. Third, interventions were specifically designed to disallow existing solution attempts which were seen as contributing to the problem. Common-sense strategies for dealing with anxiety (such as relaxation training or cognitive restructuring) were avoided — not because they were seen as inferior to the chosen interventions in some absolute sense, but because they closely resembled the basic thrust of the existing solution attempts on the part of Jill and her parents. Fourth, a one-down, collaborative practitioner style was employed to promote cooperation in implementing interventions, and client ownership of successes.

The majority of literature on strategic intervention has been written by non-school professionals dealing with non-school problems. However, the BSFI approach presented here offers several advantages for school professionals. The possibility of resolving difficult problems in a limited time period is quite appealing to school personnel, who typically consider time their most limited resource. Further, the acceptance and utilization of others' beliefs helps to foster a productive, collaborative relationship between school personnel and parents. In addition to increasing the likelihood of the acceptability and implementation of interventions, a collaborative relationship empowers parents and students to claim rightful ownership of desired changes that occur.

The systemic perspective of BSFI, which acknowledges that small changes in any aspect of a problem situation can initiate problem resolution, may be quite useful to school helping professionals who sometimes complain of restricted intervention opportunities (limited availability of parents for meetings, etc). Although every reasonable attempt is made to work with those individuals seen as most directly involved in the problem, the systemic and strategic aspects of BSFI imply that working with anyone connected to the problem can effectively alter it. Finally, the few reports of empirical investigations of strategic intervention in schools have been encouraging.

References

Kazdin, A. E. (1982) *Single-case research designs: Methods for clinical and applied settings.* New York: Oxford Press.

Kratochwill, T. R. (1985) 'Case study research in school psychology', *School Psychology Review*, 14, 204-215.

NOTE: These references are used in the excerpt above. The complete paper has more references, many of which are in the references section of this book.

9   CASE EXAMPLE —
Building on exceptions

The following paper was published in *Family Therapy Case Studies, 1990, 5(1), 3–14* and is reprinted here with permission of the author.

THE GIRL WITH THE KNOW–HOW:

Finding solutions to a school problem*

Kate Kowalski

Families frequently present to therapists with problems that occur primarily in their child's school. Not surprisingly, parents feel helpless to do anything about difficulties that occur away from home. In this case, a 12-year-old girl has been described as having difficulties applying herself and co-operating in class. An approach which uses the solution-focused ideas of de Shazer and his colleagues uses a small, and seemingly insignificant, comment on which to build a view of a solution to the problem. When difficulties at home are also raised, the emerging solution provides a base for discussing this, as well as allowing some consideration of parents' management styles.

---

*   *This case was seen while the author was a faculty member at the Brief Family Therapy Center in Milwaukee, Wisconsin. Parts of this case were described, in an abbreviated form, in Kowalski and Kral (1989).*

Kate Kowalski now works at the University of Wisconsin in Milwaukee.

Julie, aged 12, came for therapy accompanied by her mother, Maria, upon referral from the counsellor at Julie's school. Julie's family comprised her mother, her father, Joe, and 15-year-old sister, Jenny. Joe attended the third of the four sessions, while Jenny did not come to any.

I spent the first several minutes of the session socializing with Julie and Maria, finding out that Julie was in sixth grade at school and spent some time in a special class for children with learning difficulties. She had several pets and cared for a couple of horses which belonged to a neighbour in their rural-like suburb. Maria worked part-time as a clerk in a grocery store and Joe was a groundskeeper.

First session

Julie seemed quite nervous about talking with me. She was soft-spoken and frequently hid her face behind her jacket. Maria was clearly frustrated by the difficulties which led them to seek counselling, frequently throwing her hands in the air as she described her concerns. After getting to know them a bit, I asked Julie if she knew what brought them to see me.

Julie: Well, I don't really like school.
Kate: Uh mmm, how's that a problem?
Julie: Well, I'm in a special class, and ...
Maria: She's in a learning disabled class and whenever demands are put upon her she will not do them ... studying. She's gotten progressively worse. I was at school yesterday and the teacher says she doesn't raise her hand to talk in class, she doesn't *(sounding more frustrated)* ... she talks out of line, she's rude to the teacher, she won't cooperate.
Kate: And is this the first you've heard about it, or is it something ...
Maria: No, I've been trying to deal with it. But I just don't know what to do any more. And we're all very unhappy over the situation. The teacher doesn't know what to do any more, I don't know what to do any more, and I don't think Julie knows what to do any more. One day she'll be very good in class.
Julie: *(softly)* Like today.

Maria: And then there will be days on end where she just will not do any-
          thing. She becomes frustrated so easy and ...
Kate: (*interrupting*) Now wait a minute, did I hear you say that there are
          some days where she participates and does okay, ... like today?
Julie: Yeah.

My approach to therapy has been influenced a great deal by the solution-
focused model developed by the team at the Brief Family Therapy Center
(BFTC) in Milwaukee (de Shazer, 1985, 1988; de Shazer *et al*, 1986). The
BFTC team emphasizes the importance of utilizing the clients' existing solution-oriented behaviour, which they call 'exceptions'. Exceptions are those
bits of the clients' behaviour or experience which are inconsistent with the
problem description. In the case of Julie and her mum, I was interested in
how soon into the session a very useful exception became available, that of
the 'good days'. Within Maria's explanation of how bad things had been
recently, she off-handedly commented (out of frustration) that sometimes
Julie had good days, to which Julie added, 'like today'.

In using an approach which seeks to build upon those bits of experience
which are already occurring within the clients' repertoire, Maria's statement
is precisely the kind of information for which I am listening. Once an exception is identified, the process of therapy then becomes one of questioning
about the *differences* between the 'exception behaviour' and the 'problem
behaviour'.

Kate: Really?! What's um, ... tell me what's different about days like
          today.
Julie: (*shrugs her shoulders*)
Kate: How do you get them to happen?
Julie: They just happen.
Kate: They just happen? How is a day like today different from other
          days that maybe aren't so good?
          (*No response*)
Kate: I mean, if I had two video tapes and one was you in your class
          today and the other was you in your class on a not-so-good day,
          how would I know which one was you today?

Julie: Well ... *(softly)* some days my mind tells me to be good and some days it doesn't.

Kate: I'm sorry, I didn't quite get that. Some days what?

Julie: My mind tells me to be good and some days it doesn't.

Kate: Oh, really?!

Julie: Uh mmm.

Kate: What are you doing differently when you're being good?

Julie: Behave ...

Kate: Yeah.

Julie: ... raise my hand.

Kate: Raise your hand?

Julie: Yeah.

Kate: Okay. What else?

Julie: Don't talk out.

Kate: And, what do you do instead of talking out?

Julie: Sit there and raise my hand.

Kate: Um hum. Okay, so is that the main thing?

Julie: Yeah.

Kate: Okay, now I just want to make sure that I understand what the good days are like ... compared to the bad, okay? So on the good days you might raise your hand ...

Julie: Uh mmm. And we might have an easy assignment.

Kate: And you answer questions?

Julie: Uh mmm.

Kate: And you don't talk out of turn ... like you wait until ...

Julie: ... the teacher can get to me.

Kate: You do?

Julie: Uh mmm.

Kate: What else?

Julie: If it's an easy assignment I'll do it right away, if it's hard I might bring it home.

Kate: Okay, so you're more likely to do your assignments?

Julie: Yeah.

I was impressed with how readily Julie was able to describe the ways in which she behaved differently on what were described as 'good days', as well as the fact that she seemed to have some sense of her own agency in creating these days. Her comment, 'some days my mind tells me to be good and some days it doesn't' seemed to indicate that she saw herself as having some influence over her behaviour. After all, in order for her actually to have 'good days', she must, at least sometimes, listen to what she has to say to herself. I chose not to elaborate on this point directly at this time, but to do so indirectly by continuing to phrase my questions in such a way as to imply a sense of agency on her part.

After spending a little more time discussing the 'good days', particularly how often they came about and what Julie's teacher would say was different about her on these days, I decided to begin to create a frame for looking at how Maria and Julie imagined the future would be when this problem was no longer a part of their lives. In discussing an orientation towards the future, Durrant and Kowalski (1990) point out that a number of therapists have suggested approaches to questioning that include this sort of focus (for example, Lipchik, 1988; Penn, 1985; Tomm, 1987) and cite O'Hanlon and Weiner-Davis's definition of 'future oriented questions' as being where 'clients are asked to envision a future without the problem and describe what that looks like' and suggest that 'the mere act of constructing a vision of the solution acts as a catalyst for bringing it about' (1989, p. 106.).

Kate: Now let's say sometime in the future that you look back and say, 'us going and talking with Kate, that helped, that made a difference' ...

Maria: Uh mmm.

Kate: What will be happening differently that you'll be able to say that things are better?

Maria: Well, I guess, even like when I, um, will say 'well, okay, fine, now it's time that we should do our homework', or 'in fifteen minutes ... ', I've tried this, 'in fifteen minutes, when you're done watching *The Brady Bunch*, we will do your homework' and she'll just say 'okay fine, that'll be fine, Mum'. But I never hear that, it's always, 'yeah later, yeah later', or 'I don't have to', or 'you can't make me', or 'I don't want to'.

Kate: Okay. So an example will be that, when things are better, Julie will say, 'okay' and she'll do her homework?

Maria: Yeah.

Kate: Okay ... On her own, or with you?

Maria: Oh, it would be nice on her own, but I would do it with her.

Kate: Has Julie ever done her homework on her own?

Maria: Well, up until fifth grade in the L.D. program, they never really had that much homework ... it was all done at school. Last year, (to Julie) did you have homework last year? Not that much. I think it's more. And I know that the teachers are trying ... they've told me they're trying to make her more independent, that once you get into the higher grades you have to be able to do it on your own. And I realize this is a hard transition, but I find it insurmountable right now.

Kate: Okay. So one of the things that will be different is that Julie will be doing her homework?

Maria: Uh mmm.

Kate: What else will be different?

Maria: It seems like whenever our family gets together, the four of us, and we're gonna go someplace, there's ... someone is always, there's something always to argue about, that we never leave the house all happy saying, 'this is fine'. There always seems to be some little problem or some big problem or the clothes aren't right or someone's sitting at the wrong window ...

Julie: Yeah, but where do we ever go?

Maria: Well, if we go, even to church and it's the three of us, you always have to sit in the front seat and will roll the window down and her older sister will sit in the back seat and want the window rolled up, and Julie won't change places with her and Jenny's yelling because her hair's getting messed up, and it's always like that. And who gives in? Not Julie ... most of the time.

Kate: So what will be happening differently then when things are better ... in situations like that?

Maria: Well maybe they'll say to each other, and say 'okay, Jenny you sit in the front seat and keep the window rolled up or roll the window down and I don't care if my head gets messed up'.

Kate: So the sisters, they'd be, they'll be compromising more.

Maria: Yeah.

Kate: What else?

It is often tempting to become distracted by clients' description of the behaviours or problems they want to change, but it is important to persist in encouraging them to imagine the desired state. Many clients find this very difficult since they are used to thinking about themselves and the problem in a certain way and unaccustomed to talking in specific terms about how they want things to be different.

I used the examples Julie and Maria nominated to seek out further exceptions. Future oriented questions are useful in this regard in that they can serve as another pathway for identifying already existing solution-directed behaviours.

As is often the case when pursuing a solution-focus, clients begin spontaneously to offer additional examples of exceptions to the complaint. In this case, Maria told me about other examples of Julie's ability to be responsible.

Maria: Now I know several of our friends have younger kids and she's so responsible and she babysits for them and takes care of the children ...

Kate: Julie does?!

Maria: Yeah!

Kate: Oh, great!

Maria: And she's so responsible that way and I'm always amazed and I think that's really wonderful.

Kate: Wow! Yeah!

Maria: But then ... the next thing she can be so stubborn and so blockheaded that she just won't do stuff for me.

Kate: So Julie knows how to be responsible?

Maria: Yeah!

Kate: Not only look after herself, but also look after other kids?

Maria: Yes, definitely.

Kate: Wow! That's great!

Maria: It is!

Kate: Yeah! Did you know that you Mum thought that you were responsible?

Julie: No, she never told me.

Kate: Are you surprised to hear it?

Julie: Yes.

Kate: Do you think of yourself as being responsible?

Julie: No.

Kate: You don't?

Julie: No.

Kate: How come?

Julie: 'cos, no-one ever tells me I am.

Kate: Do you think doing stuff like babysitting and taking such good care of these kids, does that seem to you to be something a responsible person does?

Julie: Yes.

Kate: Yeah? And you do do that, huh, ... I mean your Mum's not making that up, is she?

Julie: No, tomorrow I have a babysitting job at night.

Kate: Oh yeah?!

Julie: Yeah!

Kate: Wow!

I thought it interesting that Maria began to broaden her frame for viewing Julie's behaviour by suggesting Julie's babysitting as demonstrating her ability to be responsible. Thus, the description moved away from Julie's ability to have 'good days' at school to her ability to be 'responsible'.

I went on to ask Julie how she got to be so responsible, a self-description she now seemed to be entertaining. Interestingly, she replied that her mother taught her.

Summary message: Building up to noticing more

After taking my 'think break', consulting with the supervisee behind the one-way mirror, I delivered my summary message.

Kate: Let me tell you what I've been thinking about. Um, I should tell you that we're really impressed with the both of you ... *(Mum looks surprised)* which you may find surprising to hear because I know how frustrating this whole situation is.

Julie: *(interrupts)* Very!

Kate: *(to Julie)* You can tell, huh?!

Kate: But, Maria, you're clearly a very caring and concerned and conscientious mother

Julie: *(interrupts)* She is.

Kate: ... who truly wants ... and Julie knows it ... who truly wants the best for Julie.

Maria: *(crying)* I do.

Kate: Yeah, and that's real obvious.

(Julie pats Mum's arm)

Kate: And we're certainly struck with how you've raised her to be a responsible girl in some very significant ways. She takes good care of the animals.

Maria: She does.

Kate: She's a good babysitter ... something a lot of kids her age, no matter how good they are in other areas, wouldn't be able to handle ... they wouldn't be responsible enough to handle it. And ...

Maria: I know! If I say to someone, 'Julie's giving me a hard time right now', they're flabbergasted, 'you can't mean that', they would expect it of my older daughter because she's very flighty and not responsible, and ...

Kate: And I'm sure that's what makes it all the harder because you know that in a lot of areas Julie is responsible and can be. That's not something she knows about herself, but that's something you know about her.

Maria: Uh mmm.

Kate: And it's clear that you invest a lot of yourself in trying to help her. And I think that's neat ... I think there are a lot of parents who would just say , 'what can I do?', and be very apathetic about it.

Maria: That's not good enough for me.

Kate: And Julie, we were thinking about how open and honest you are, and you were in talking with me today. And I think that's especially neat because it's hard to come and talk to someone you don't know. ... And you strike me as someone who speaks her mind, and I think that's neat. I talk with a lot of kids your age and a lot of them are shy and afraid to talk and who don't say what's on their mind, but you're somebody who knows how to say what she thinks ... I think that's neat. The other thing I was thinking about is how ... not amazed, that would be too strong a word, but I think it's pretty neat that you know how to have good days. Do you know what I mean?

Julie: Yeah!

Kate: You know how to have good days at school because you do it sometimes ... you already said that two times this week you did. And that sometimes you can get your mind to tell you to be good, and that's pretty amazing. And I'm curious about that 'cos I'm not sure exactly how you do it ... how you get your mind to tell you to be good, and then not only does your mind tell you it, but you actually do it ... that's pretty amazing. And I would like to know some more about how you get that to happen, okay. So you're not going to like this, but this isn't going to be too bad, I'm going to give you a little bit of homework.

Maria: *(laughs)*

Kate: This really isn't bad kind of homework. Okay? Maybe I shouldn't even call it homework, maybe we should call it an experiment or something. What I want you to do ... are you listening?

Julie: Yeah, I'm listening.

Kate: I want you to pay real, real close attention to the next time that you have a good day. Okay?

Julie: Like tomorrow!

Kate: Like tomorrow ... I want you to pay attention to how you get yourself to have a good day, okay?

Julie: Okay!

Kate: ... and I want you to pay attention to how your teacher reacts and how your Mum and Dad react.

Julie: Okay.

Kate: Okay?

Julie: Yep!

Kate: If you've got a good memory, keep it in your head, otherwise if it
          helps, write it down 'cos I'm going to ask you about it when we
          get together next week.

Julie: Okay.

Kate: What I'd like for you to do, Maria, and you may want to involve
          you husband in doing this too, is to watch for signs that Julie is
          going to have a good day and what's different about her that tells
          you that, 'oh, she's going to have a good day today' ... when
          you're able to predict it.

Maria: Uh mmm.

Kate: Umm. and don't talk to one another about it ... each of you do
          these things on your own, okay?

Maria: Okay.

In summarising the session, I wanted to build on the 'new' information
which Julie and Maria now seemed to be entertaining about themselves in
relation to the problem. In leading up to my suggested task, it seemed important to tell them both how impressed I was with their efforts — which I was!
While it is ultimately most important that the clients come to appreciate
their own efforts and accomplishments, I believe clients find it helpful to
have these acknowledged by the therapist. I was moved by Maria's tearful
response to what I had considered very straight-forward comments about my
view of her as a 'caring, concerned and conscientious mother'. The observational tasks (de Shazer and Molnar, 1984) were designed to continue to
focus Julie and Maria's attention toward the exceptions rather than the problems, so as to build upon what had already been working.

Second session — ten days later

I began this meeting by asking Julie how she had been managing to have
good days at school. In doing 'brief' therapy, I find it helpful to structure
questions in such a way as to assume change in the direction of the solution.
In keeping with this rule of thumb my question to Julie was one that implicitly suggested that she had been continuing to have good days, and that it

was she who did something to create them.

Julie came over and stood beside me to show me the notebook in which her teachers had written comments about her behaviour. It was evident that she was feeling quite proud of herself as she flipped through the pages and I read aloud the comments. They included such statements as, 'Julie is trying to show some restraint, hope she keeps it up'; 'great day, lovely child, very cooperative, she can do it!'; 'much better'; 'settled down nicely, followed directions, I sure hope this continues'; 'good day, followed directions, worked hard'; 'not bad, held it together, self-control is the name of the game'; 'what a girl, six great days, she's the sunshine of my life!'. I found the difference in Julie's demeanour to be quite remarkable. She was noticeably more confident, which I guessed reflected the greater sense of self-control she was feeling.

The change in Maria's appearance was equally dramatic. Whereas in the first session she had seemed drawn, frustrated, and overwhelmed, she now looked very animated, cheerful, and proud of Julie's accomplishments.

I congratulated Julie and asked that she fill me in on how she had done it.

Julie: When my teacher tells me that I did something too sloppy and I had to do it over, I tell myself I have to do it, and my mom would yell, and I don't get a treat when I get home.

Kate: So, you were talking to yourself a lot, huh?

Julie: I do that a lot.

Kate: And you were listening.

Julie: Yeah.

Kate: Is that new, is that different?

Julie: No, I always did that.

Kate: You always did that. You always what, talk to yourself?

Julie: And if I don't listen, I yell at myself!

Maria: You do?!

Julie: Uh hmm.

Kate: So what's different now that you're talking to yourself, listening, and you're doing it?

Julie: My math teacher's nice now ...

Kate: Yeah.

Julie: Cos, like if I have a good day, and I come in the next day, she's
           happy 'cos I had a great day the other day. Then it keeps going.
Kate: So tell me, did you find out that the more good days you had the
           more you felt like having good days?
Julie: Um hmm.
Kate: So are you finding out you like good days better than bad days?
Julie: Um hmm.
Kate: How come, what's better about having good days?
Julie: Now my L.D. teacher, Mrs. Cavanough, if I'm good and other kids
           aren't, and I see how she yells at them, and I don't want to be like
           that.
Kate: What made you decide that?
Julie: 'cos they make a fool of themselves! And I don't want to.

At this point I asked Maria, who was grinning from ear to ear as Julie
commented on her accomplishments, what she made of it all. She said she
wasn't sure what made a difference and, in an attempt to put things together,
began to tell me about a particular morning when Julie had a tantrum before
school. Julie interrupted to remind her mum that, while the morning had
begun on a bad note, she had a talk to herself on the way to school and
ended up having a good day. I was especially curious at this bit of news
since, in my experience, taking what starts off being a difficult day and turning it into a good one is no easy feat.

When I asked Maria how successfully she had been able to predict the
good days, she replied that she had been wrong that morning. In an attempt
to avoid getting hung up on this one 'glitch' in an otherwise good period, I
persisted asking Maria about the other days. Her enthusiastic reply was,
'well, she was good!'.

We spent the remainder of the session highlighting Julie's new behaviours, and Maria's new responses. At first Maria commented that she didn't
think she was doing anything different. While I was convinced that this was
probably not the case, I thought it best to avoid challenging her on the point
and instead asked what she noticed Julie doing differently. This then led to a
series of questions about Maria's responses to Julie's successes. With this,
Maria came to say that she, in fact, was doing some things differently – set-

ting much clearer limits, avoiding getting caught in futile arguments with Julie, rewarding her for her efforts and successes, and offering various encouraging comments.

While Maria was obviously very pleased with Julie's progress at school, she continued to have some concern about the fighting and bickering that occurred at home between Julie and her sister. I saw this as a potential 'red herring', which would best be avoided so that a focus on this problem would not detract from our focus on Julie's success and their beginning to envision a different future. Nonetheless, I felt it important at least to acknowledge Maria's concern by spending a few moments discussing it, and then suggested that we put this issue 'on hold' for a time in order not to diminish Julie's sense of her success at school and to further encourage her efforts. Maria readily agreed with this suggestion.

I ended the session by complimenting Julie on her ability to take her own advice, as it was clear that she had a lot of very useful things to say to herself. I also said that I was particularly impressed by the fact that she not only had good things to tell herself, but also she was smart enough to listen. Julie seemed to enjoy being thought of as smart and readily agreed with my comment! I told Maria that I was impressed by her ability to predict and reward Julie for the 'good days'.

I also remarked on an incident which they had told me had occurred during the previous week in which Maria reminded Julie she had a science test and encouraged her to study for it. Julie's response had been that she had already studied and knew the material. I suggested that, in the past, Maria would have insisted that Julie prove she knew the material but this time had resisted the temptation and allowed Julie to judge for herself. It seemed Maria somehow wisely and intuitively knew that one of the things Julie was learning now was how to be more responsible for herself and that, in order to learn this, she would need to be given opportunities to practice. Maria was quite receptive to this idea and agreed to my suggestion that she continue to notice ways in which Julie was taking more and more responsibility. My only suggestion to Julie was that she continue to notice how she managed to have good days at school. We scheduled another appointment for two weeks time.

Third session

This meeting involved Julie, Maria, and Joe. Maria and I had previously discussed the possibility of Joe joining us, especially considering his concern over the fighting and bickering between the two girls. He seemed quite happy to participate in the session in spite of his stated reservations about going outside the home and family for assistance. I thanked him for coming and said I felt it would be helpful to understand his perspective on things since he was obviously a very important part of Julie's life.

I began by asking how things had been going since our last meeting and everyone agreed that Julie was continuing to do very well at school. They all seemed very pleased about this, and Julie told me how happy her teacher was, too. I asked Joe about the kinds of changes he noticed in Julie and he talked about how pleasant it was to come home and hear about the positive things Julie was doing at school rather than about problems.

In spite of all this, it was clear that Maria and Joe were still concerned about the fighting between Julie and her sister and that they saw Julie as being the primary instigator of these difficulties. In beginning to address this issue and their responses to it, it became increasingly evident that Joe and Maria had quite different ideas about how to approach problems which arose with the girls' behaviour. Given this, I thought it best that we discuss parenting issues without Julie in the room. When children are overtly aware of their parents' differences, they are more likely, sometimes inadvertently and sometimes purposely, to play on them, which often results in further disagreement between the parents. Moreover, discussing these kinds of differences is often quite difficult for a couple and even moreso in front of their children. They seemed relieved by the suggestion that we spend a few moments talking about 'adult stuff' and Julie accepted that she should not be part of this.

We spent quite a bit of time discussing the ideas each of them had about how to handle the girls' fighting. Joe volunteered that he tended to take a more 'hard-line' approach, jumping in fairly quickly and basically ordering the girls to stop. This seemed to work temporarily, but not in the long-term. Maria said her approach was a bit more 'calm' in that she would try to talk with the girls and get them to work it out by talking. This seemed to work sometimes, but not always. While both parents said they were frustrated by the problem, they agreed that it was Joe who had the most trouble coping with it. Recently, his reaction had been simply to retreat, either leaving the room and going to another part of the house, or leaving the house and going for a walk or drive. This left Maria feeling more and more frustrated with Joe and the girls as she felt rejected and put down for her parenting.

We went on to talk not only about their different styles, but also the differences between their daughters. They both agreed that Jenny seemed, in general, to respond quite well to Maria's 'looser, more casual' approach, while Julie seemed to require a bit more firmness and structure. Maria, in fact, began to recall a couple of times recently when she took a more 'bottom-line' type of approach with Julie and the positive results it promoted. I concluded my time with them by stating that I saw it as fortunate that Maria and Joe had different areas of expertise to offer their children and that each of them seemed quite skilled in some very important aspects of parenting. I suggested that, rather than viewing their differences as a problem, it might be more helpful for us to view them as a resource for them in assisting the girls to become responsible young women. At this point in their lives, Julie seemed to benefit most from a more firm, straight-forward approach, while Jenny seemed to respond well to things being a bit looser. I left them with the suggestion that they notice what they saw in the others' approach that seemed to work with each of their daughters, to which they agreed.

I then saw Julie on her own and spent most of the time talking about how she was continuing to do well at school. We briefly discussed what ideas she had about fighting less with Jenny, and this led Julie to give several examples of times she could have started arguments, but stopped herself. I was curious about her ability and decision to do this and suggested that she might want to notice how she got herself to resist the temptation to fight with Jenny. We decided to get together again in about three weeks time.

Between sessions phone call

About ten days later I received a phone call from Maria who was very concerned about several really awful days Julie had had at school. Maria was very concerned that they were 'back at square one' and had lost all the progress Julie had made. She was again feeling defeated and overwhelmed, and was generally confused about what happened to cause this turn of events. I reassured Maria that, while this appeared to be a set-back, it seemed to me to be quite normal and natural given the impressive changes Julie had been making. I apologized for having been so swept away with how well things had been going that I neglected to caution the family that occasionally the problem fights back. I also said that often, when children are learning to become more responsible, they need to test themselves a bit in order to make sure they can get themselves 'back on track'. Maria seemed relieved to hear all of this and readily accepted my apology and way of thinking. I suggested that there had been a number of very helpful strategies Maria used in helping Julie early on and encouraged her to continue to try these. I assured Maria that I would be happy to meet with them again prior to our next scheduled meeting if she thought that necessary. She said she would keep that in mind, but for now she was happy to deal with this on her own.

Fourth session — our final meeting

This session took place as scheduled and included Maria and Julie. Not knowing what to expect, I was pleased to see that they both looked happy and relaxed. I was also struck with how confident Julie looked and sounded as we began joking about how 'off track' things had been for a while.

Maria: Boy, things were terribly off track for a while! *(laughing)*

Kate: Yeah? But I take it now it's back on track.

Julie: Oh yeah!

Kate: How did you get it back on track?

Julie: My teacher told me I had to.

Kate: Yeah. So what made you decide to listen?

        (pause)

Maria: It seems so long ago, doesn't it?

Kate: You mean you've been on track for awhile?

Julie: Yeah.

Maria: I don't remember what day I talked to you, but the next day after that she was better.

Maria then told me about the conversation they had had that afternoon when she picked Julie up from school and reminded her of our appointment. She said she had to laugh when Julie responded with, 'Why? What is she doing for our family?!' I found this comment amusing myself and saw it as a clear sign that Julie knew it was she who was creating the changes in her life and not me. We spent a few minutes talking and joking about who was 'doing the most' to help Julie have good days. The consensus was that it was well and truly Julie who was responsible for her change in direction.

Guessing that this would probably be our last meeting, I asked a number of questions to help mark the changes Julie and the family had made.

Kate: So what's been happening that you want to see continue?

Maria: Well, let's see. Julie has good days at school!

Kate: She does?!

Julie: Yeah, and the other day she *(pointing to mum)* brought me a big cake.

Maria: *(interrupting)* and I didn't even know for sure that she was going to have a good day because she left really crabby. But she had a good day even after she left really crabby.

Kate: Wow!

Julie: Oh, I always do.

Kate: So you assumed that she would know how to turn it around?

Maria: Yep. But I kept the cake in the car because she had to stay up in her room until her Dad got home because she was really bad. She stayed up there until her Dad got home and when I read in her notebook from school that she had a good day, I thought, 'well, then I'll get the cake out!'

After discussing the Halloween decorations on the cake, how good it was, and how the whole family benefited from Julie's good day, we went on to talk about the other things that had been happening that the family found pleasing. Maria said that everyone seemed to be getting along better at home, that there was less fighting, and that Joe had been more involved in helping with the girls. She told me some of the ways in which she was dealing with Julie that seemed to be helping her learn to be more responsible, such as being firmer and clearer about what she expected, as well as encouraging her when she did something responsible.

We proceeded with another question I frequently ask in a final session:

Kate: So tell me, is this good stuff going to last?
Julie: Well, I hope so.
Kate: Yeah ...
Julie: Yeah, I think so.
Kate: So you think this is going to last? You think you know what to do to keep this good stuff going?
Julie: Oh, yeah!

I asked Julie a scaling question (Kowalski and Kral, 1989) to assess how confident she was feeling with regard to continuing to have good days. On a scale from zero to ten, she rated her confidence level at nine, saying, 'well, I know I may have a bad day sometimes, but I hope I only have one!'. This seemed to me to be quite a realistic view.

Kate: And do you think that when you have a bad day you'll know how to get back into having more good days?
Julie: Well, yeah, 'cos I can only have one!
Kate: What do you think is the main thing, the most important thing that you can do to help keep the good days coming?
Julie: Well the only thing I have to do is listen to my teacher and do it because I know if I don't do it, then I don't get it, and I get frustrated, and I get a time out, and I get more mad, and I talk really mean to them, and I usually end up in the office!
Kate: So the most important thing is to listen to your teachers and do what they ask you to do?
Julie: Yeah, 'cos that would lead to a lot of problems if I didn't.
Maria: When did you figure this all out?
Julie: When I was in the corner!
Maria: Oh, I've been trying to tell you that for years, Julie.
Julie: I know, I listen to myself now!

Kate: Are you surprised that she's listening to herself and figuring this all out?

Maria: Well, I bet I've told her that same line hundreds of times.

Kate: Sure. I think it's something that Julie had to learn for herself. *(Julie and mum laugh)*

Maria: I'm just amazed!

Kate: And all of a sudden, whatever it took, Julie decided that she can start listening to herself, and she has good things to say to herself, a lot of which she learned from you.

Maria: *(laughing)* I can't believe it, this is just amazing. I'm so proud of you! That's really neat!

I then asked Maria how confident she was using the same scale. Her response was '7 $1/2$', which I framed as indicating a 'healthy bit of caution'. Julie was less than thrilled with her mother's response and jokingly tried to persuade her to increase the rating. In order to help Julie see that there was hope her mother would become more confident, I asked Maria to imagine that in a few weeks time her response to the scaling question was '9' and what she thought would have happened between now and then. She said that Julie having two weeks of good days at school would make a difference. Julie seemed pleased with this and went on to indicate that she had no intention of having more than one bad day for the rest of the term. This statement served to reinforce for me that Julie truly had come to see herself as having the ability to do well at being responsible.

Final comments for a final session

After taking a short 'think break' (this time working on my own), I came back and summarized my thoughts about the session.

Kate: Well, congratulations! *(Julie and Maria laugh)* Really, on your determination and 'stick-to-itiveness'! I think that's terrific. *(To Julie)* Do you know what that means, 'stick-to-itiveness'?

Julie: Not really!

Kate: It means sticking to it even though it's kind of hard.

Julie: Oh, yeah!

Kate: I think that's terrific. And do you know what I'm most struck
         with?
Julie: What?
Kate: I'm most struck with the fact that you took what seemed to be a
         setback, ...
Julie: Oh, yeah.
Kate: ... you know, having several not so good days, and you turned it
         around to get back on track. And that's a hard thing to do.
Julie: Oh, not for me. Well, sometimes, but ...
Kate: See, and you took what is a hard thing for most people to do and
         made it seem pretty easy. So, what that tells me is that you must be
         pretty strong. It also tells me that you learned from the not so good
         days some really helpful stuff, like it helps to listen to yourself, to
         listen to your teacher, and that when you do, things go smoother at
         school and at home. Right?! And you've got to be pretty smart to
         figure all of that out. And you figured it out real well. And I'm
         really impressed with you, too, Maria ... the fact that you hung in
         there, even though I'm sure you were really frustrated over those
         few days and were probably really tempted to give up and start to
         think 'we're back at square one, we're back at the beginning'. But
         you didn't. You stuck with it and helped Julie turn things around
         by giving her some encouragement, by setting some firm limits, by
         saying 'this is it', and by rewarding her when she did well. I think
         that's super. Both of you are really on track. It seems to me you
         both know what you need to do, so keep doing it.

I suggested that we schedule another appointment for six weeks time that
they should cancel, assuming everything was continuing to go smoothly. In
fact, that's what happened. A few days prior to this meeting, Maria phoned
to say that all was going well and that she saw no need for this session.

Conclusion

When I talked with Julie and Maria about my teaching and whether I
might use our sessions together, Julie decided she wanted their story to have

the title 'The girl with the know-how' (hence the title of this paper). This seemed a clear statement that she believed that she had solved these difficulties herself, that she had found the 'know-how' to overcome them.

Julie's realisation of her own success demonstrates the fundamental philosophy of the solution-focused approach. The idea of exceptions to problem behaviour is that these events are *already* occurring. That is, the solution to the problem already exists in the clients' repertoire rather than being something that the therapist has to create or engineer.

Throughout this case, from the point in the first session when 'good days' were mentioned, my aim was to highlight those existing examples of self-control, responsibility and success in such a way as to allow Julie and Maria to appreciate their significance. I did not attempt to encourage Julie to try anything that she was not already doing. Similarly, when the issue of Maria and Joe's different approaches to parenting arose, I sought to offer a frame for thinking about these that allowed them to appreciate the strengths of what they were doing.

In many ways, the information I had about the situation was minimal. My initial information gathering was interrupted by the discovery of the exception, and this was more useful information than further detail of the problem. Similarly, I did not contact Julie's school for information or to offer advice. The information about 'good days' was the information that made a difference, and allowed Julie to show herself, her parents and her school that she had the know-how to be successful.

Solution-focused therapy is usually brief therapy. Building on something that is already happening is almost always briefer than attempting to create something from scratch.

References

The references from this article are included in the reference section at the end of the book.

10   RUNNING GROUPS with a COMPETENCY FOCUS

School counsellors sometimes find themselves having to conduct groups. How might we think about these from a brief therapy perspective?

Selekman (1991) has outlined the structure and process of a parents' group which operated on solution-focused therapy principles. These groups met for six weekly sessions, with group members being parents of adolescents (usually adolescents with substance abuse problems, amongst others) and each group session had a particular focus:

1. Introducing new ideas — a combination of joining a context-setting with education about core assumptions of the approach, leading to a request to look for "exceptions" in the adolescent's behaviour during the ensuing week.

2. Looking for small changes — group discussion of the exceptions and of what the parents had done (intentionally or otherwise) to help these things happen, leading to a discussion of small goals and the request to notice all the things they (parents) do towards reaching these goals.

3. What's working — group discussion and encouragement about steps parents have taken.

4. Doing something different — the group highlights changes each parent has achieved and discusses the specific parenting strategies they can derive from these successes.

5. Keeping the change happening — more highlighting and discussion of strategies that are "different".

6. Celebration — parents have a celebratory party, receive certificates, etc.

As will be seen from this brief outline, the process of the group programme follows more or less the kind of progression we might expect in a therapy case with an individual or family. The group processes are harnessed to provide more ideas, more examples to discuss, and more people to offer encouragement, however the process is not greatly different.

Mutual support is still an important ingredient of these groups, however the structure which the authors provide allows this support to be focused on success and sharing ideas, rather than just on sharing failures.

Linda Metcalf, a colleague in Arlington, Texas, has used solution-focused ideas in group therapy within both hospital and school settings.

On the following page is an example of a form used within the hospital setting, where the programme required that there be "process groups" each morning and evening. Of course, such "process groups" had typically been difficult sessions which provided an arena for anger to be vented, crises and failures to be "worked through", people to feel picked on, clients to confront one another about aspects of their behaviour, and so on. That is, the groups seemed to reflect assumptions that groups provided a context for confrontation and catharsis.

Linda's use of the forms was an effort to change the focus of the groups to one of success, with clients encouraged to discuss each other's successes and even to watch out for others being successful.

Similarly, Linda has been in settings where she was required to conduct an "anger group". Again, the existence of the group reflected assumptions that the group context would allow a safe environment for the ventilation of angry feelings. However, this was not Linda's assumption, and she developed the form (shown on the following page) to help focus the anger group towards a consideration of times when group members showed greater control.

In this case, she used White's (1988) technique of "externalising" the anger — reframing anger as something external against which the children could "fight". Thus, the content of the groups revolved around this theme, which provided a concrete way for the children to think about the effects of their anger. It allowed them to distinguish between anger "being in control"

MORNING/EVENING PROCESS GROUPS

Daily goal-setting is a way of achieving, in a short time, what's really important. These groups will meet daily.

- -

A.M. GROUP

Date: ....

Goal for today: ....

1. How have you minimally or successfully accomplished this goal in the past?

2. How were you wise enough to accomplish it in this way?

3. Of these strategies you have used before, which one will you use today?

4. On a scale of 1 – 10 ("1" being completely impossible and "10" being completely successful), where would you like to be at the end of today?

P.M. GROUP

5. On the scale in Question 4, how close did you get to your goal? How did you manage that?

6. Ask your group members what changes they noticed in you today as you moved towards your goal.

A form used in morning and evening "Process Groups" in a residential program. © 1992, Linda Metcalf. Adapted and used with permission.

ANGER GROUP

"Anger" plagues everyone once in a while. A method of venting and airing feelings, it can be a healthy release. Sometimes, however, "anger" creates problems in our lives, which distance us from others, threaten physical harm or sabotage our future plans and relationships. The "anger group" aims to help you look at times when you did not let "anger" interfere with your life. No one can be angry 100% of the time. Our aim in this group is to identify times when you were angry, but used good strategies to make sure the "anger" did not take over.

Use the chart below to help identify "triggers" anger uses and how you have prevented "anger" from attacking your life.

SITUATIONS WHICH ENCOUR-AGE ANGER TO TAKE OVER (When anger tried to control me)	SITUATIONS WHERE ANGER WAS NOT SUCCESSFUL (How I controlled anger)
1.	1. ....
2.	2. ....
3.	3. ....
4.	4. ....
5.	5. ....

A. In what situation today would you like to be more in control of your anger?

B. When was the last time you were successful at controlling it?

C. How did you do this?

D. What is your plan for today, based on how you controlled "anger" in the past?

E. On a scale of 1 to 10 (1 is "anger is completely in control" and 10 is "I am completely in control"), where are you now? ...... As you try the things that have worked before, where would you like to be by .... (tonight, this weekend, etc.)?

A form used in "Anger Groups". © 1992, Linda Metcalf.
Adapted and used with permission.

and their "controlling the anger" (which allows anger still to be present and expressed, but within a context of some degree of control).

These are both examples of fairly structured group programmes, where the structure has been altered to encourage a greater focus on competence. Again, the steps are similar to those used in counselling sessions, with the group processes used to help encourage and highlight success.

11 HIGHLIGHTING CHANGE
— and HELPING it PERSIST

Brief therapy approaches rest on the idea that we can make small changes, and that these small changes can lead (almost inevitably) to larger changes — as people behave differently, experience others responding to them differently, and so begin to think about themselves differently.

Therefore, having achieved some change, the important question becomes that of how to encourage the change to continue. Just as exceptions are often not immediately seen by the client as significant, so changes that begin to occur are not always appreciated.

Many of the same techniques as are used in initial intervention may be used subsequently to highlight changes and so encourage them to persist. Our focus continues to be on *what's happening (differently)*, however our aim is that the client will build a new view of self on these differences.

With Kate Kowalski, I have commented, in regard to clients who have experienced sexual abuse, that it is a helpful progression when the client stops thinking of her self as a "victim" and begins to see herself as a "survivor". Nonetheless, the idea of being a "survivor" still rests on seeing oneself in relation to the abuse (that which was survived) and we would hope that we can help our clients move on to new ideas about themselves, whereby they do not define themselves in relation to the abuse at all.

A similar concern might be expressed about people continuing to define themselves as "alcoholic", even many years after they stop drinking. Such a problem-centred description serves to keep the problem alive as part of the person's view of self, thus the person can never really feel that he or she has overcome the problem. That is, there remains in the individual's view of self a significant deficit or failing, which must impede the experience of competence or achievement. (Durrant & Kowalski, 1990, p. 109)

Similarly, my concern when working with the girl with an "obsessive-compulsive" problem, which had been framed as "struggling with the fears", was that she should end our meetings *not* thinking of herself as someone who could "beat" fears, but as someone who could be more independent and self-reliant. (Durrant, 1989).

Kowalski & Kral (1989) describe the importance, in subsequent sessions, after change has begun to occur, of "cheerleading" — of encouraging, complimenting and "cheering" the changes that have begun to emerge.

> In circumstances in which people are clearly motivated to change aspects of their life, we are more than happy to act as cheerleaders in respect of their attempts to be different (though we usually draw the line at wearing short skirts and waving pom-poms). (Cade & O'Hanlon, 1993, p. 68)

Certainly, there is nothing wrong with students seeing that we are pleased with the changes they have begun to make. However, this stance can sometimes present difficulties.

> If we can bring a piece of different behavior into prominence, highlight it by asking questions about it, then it will have some effect. Rather than our pronouncing the importance of a [change], it is often better to be curious about it. We can contrast it with previous behavior, ask how the person concerned makes sense of it, wonder about how he or she was able to do it, and speculate about what difference it might make. In this way, we invite the person concerned to think about the event and its meaning. Making a proclamation about success is easier and may feel better to us; however, leaving the young person and/or parents with questions that highlight the excep-

tion and its meaning may be more useful in the longer term. My colleague, Kate Kowalski, has referred to the "Colombo approach." Those familiar with the TV detective will recall his constant quizzical questions about what behavior or evidence might mean, which has the disarming effect of leaving people to figure it out for themselves. (Durrant, 1993, p. 93).

Thus, in counselling sessions, we usually ask questions, maintain a puzzled stance about change, and explore in detail the differences that any differences are (and will be) making. In this way, we hope to enlarge the differences in the client's mind (rather than in our own mind) and so maximise the possibility of their continuing.

In the case I have mentioned earlier of the girl with an "obsessive-compulsive" problem (Durrant, 1989), it became clear in the third session that changes were evident but that Sarah was responding non-chalantly to my questions about what these changes meant. Finally, I asked, "If someone who has not seen you for some time, and so does not even know that you had this problem, sees you in the next couple of weeks, what do you think that person will notice that is different?".

When clients do not seem to appreciate the significance of changes, it can be helpful to ask them to speculate about what other people (teachers, parents, others) will notice. The fact of imagining and describing these changes seems to make them more likely to occur. In this example, the question invited Sarah to "move beyond" the changes directly related to the problem and begin to speculate about how they were 'generalised".

Awards and certificates

Schools (particularly primary schools) are well-used to giving awards to children in weekly assemblies. In my own childrens' school, class awards are often given for improved performance rather than for excellence. Such awards are clearly meaningful for the children concerned, however we should not overlook the fact that they are meaningful for teachers (and other students) as well.

Eastwood Family Therapy Centre
P.O. Box 630, EPPING NSW 2121

This is to certify that

Amy McIntosh

has achieved an outstanding performance in

Pushing herself

Not giving in to scared feelings

Learning to rely on herself

Dated this 10th day of February, 1993

Certficicate given to 11-year-old girl who presented with difficulties of going to school, and some sleeping problems. Exceptions were framed as times she "relied on herself", and counselling built on this.

That is, if a particular student receives an award, publicly, for (for example) "a great effort in controlling her temper", this is not only an encouragement for the child concerned but is also more likely to encourage school staff to notice any further examples of "temper control". The award itself has obvious reinforcement benefits. Moreover, it is likely to lead to staff talking to the child about examples of "temper control". Such interactions will not only affect the child's view of her own ability to curb her temper, but will also have a profound affect on the way that teachers respond to her. The more they respond to the child as someone who is able to control her temper, the more likely she is to be able to do so, and so the more likely the changes are to continue.

In my therapy practice, I often give certificates for such things as "Champion Grower Upper", "Expert Temper Fighter", "Learning to rely on himself", and so on. Whilst the children who receive them usually seem pleased, it is also interesting the number of times that they seem to have a profound effect on their parents as well.

Reporting on difference

Another way to help consolidate changes that have begun to emerge is to involve the student and/or family in reporting on these to others. In my own practice, I often ask my clients to help me write reports to the people or agency that referred them to me.

Thus, an interview might be spent reviewing the changes that have occurred, highlighting the particular things that have been done differently, and speculating on what other people might notice. The writing of the report or letter provides a focus for reviewing and highlighting the changes.

Recording and celebrating change

Awards and certificates are one way that changes may be highlighted, and celebrated. Once acknowledged publicly, change is more likely to continue. The certificate becomes a permanent record, a reminder of success.

We might use many of the kinds of activities that are common in schools to help record and celebrate change. I have described elsewhere a variety of celebrations and "ritual" ways of marking change in the residential setting (Durrant, 1993) and similar ideas may be employed in the school.

- Certificates and awards — either presented to the student or displayed in the classroom (This is more helpful than displaying a behaviour modification chart in the classroom, since this may become a display of *lack* of success).

- Speeches that review change — essentially a review of exceptions, or of small steps that have been achieved towards solution.

- Students being asked to draw a picture, or write a story, showing how things are different (more useful than asking them to draw the problem). Or, students might be asked to draw or write about how the future will be different, now things have begun to change.

- Class parties, convened specifically to celebrate the end of a problem (or the achievement of a specific step towards its solution).

- Ritual disposal (burning or burying) of something that symbolizes the problem.

- Giving a small gift to symbolize the change (a baseball cap for a student who has stopped "striking out")

- White and Epston (1989) give many examples of the use of letters and other written communication to highlight change and encourage people to continue to think differently about themselves, many of which might provide ideas for use in schools.

Some may be concerned that the public use of these ideas, in front of the other children, might be embarrassing for the student. Nonetheless, most students are aware of other student's problems that are displayed in class or playground, and such public recognition of change may have an impact on them as well.

12   CONSULTING to TEACHERS

One of the important roles of the School Counsellor is to consult to class teachers and school executives about particular students, often with a request that some kind of programme will be designed to be used in the classroom. Since counsellors have limited time and resources, they are not able to conduct counselling sessions with every student who is identified as a problem and must often work indirectly, through others.

A brief therapy approach is essentially a collaborative approach, where the counsellor does not seek to set him or herself up as an "expert who can fix things", and so is usually marked by a cooperative relationship between counsellor and client. Thus, the approach is well-suited to the demands of consulting to teachers and many of the ideas and techniques already discussed may be used when talking with teachers.

In many situations, it is the teacher who is the "client" for the intervention anyway — he or she has decided that things need to be different. At the same time, however, the teacher is a colleague and is likely to react with annoyance if he or she thinks the counsellor is "trying to do therapy on me". Fortunately, most of the ideas we have discussed are commonsense and can be expressed in language that is not the language of therapy.

Therefore, we may employ strategies such as reframing, questioning about exceptions, prescribing "doing something different", and so on, with the teachers to whom we consult. These may be employed in the context of informal, collegial chats. As with the counselling situation, the teacher needs to feel that the counsellor has understood and appreciated how difficult the situation is. Only then is cooperation likely. During the discussion, the counsellor needs to be alert to any details which might suggest a solution and which might be able to be encouraged or built upon. Teachers are much more likely to be successful in changing a child's behaviour if they see the strategy as having come from themselves. A strategy simply given by the counsellor may be less likely to work, since it may remind the teacher that he or she was not smart enough/professional enough/skilled enough, etc. to solve the problem.

- That sounds incredibly frustrating. It seems like he's dominating the classroom nearly all of the time. Tell me, when was the last time he seemed to pull his head in even a little? (Really? What do you think you were doing that made that happen?

- I can see why you dread Year 9. I was wondering when you would say the last time was that you felt a little more on top of things with them? (Okay? What was different that day?)

- The worst kid you have ever had! She certainly sounds like it. Now, I remember your telling me about a kid last term who was nearly as bad. Yes, that's right, Susie. Remind me, what strategies were you able to develop for handling Susie? (How did you manage to do that? What difference did it make? If you were to try something similar with Renee, how confident do you think you could be?)

- So, the day you were feeling sick, Robert seemed to back off a little? That's interesting. Isn't it funny how sometimes kids seem to sense these things and even respond appropriately? So, I never realised Robert could be that sensitive. Maybe that's a side of him we haven't noticed before. In fact, maybe it's a side of him that he hasn't noticed much! I wonder if we could figure out a way to help the sensitive side of him get bigger?

- Trudy? Isn't she the girl you sent to give me that message the other day? From what you've said about her, it must have taken some trust to let her out of your sight while she brought me the message. How did you manage that? Did it pay off? (So she seemed to respond to being given extra responsibility? Maybe we could harness that?)

- Okay, so you have no idea what to do with Year 11. Tell me, in your years of teaching, how have you handled unmotivated classes in the past? What's the most successful thing you ever did with kids of that kind? What's the most outrageous thing you ever did?

Questions such as these seek to elicit information about past and current successes. They should be explored gently and without giving the slightest impression of "see, this problem isn't as bad as you say". The questions might include examples of reframing (such as the "sensitive student") and may lead to specific things that have worked and can be tried again, or may lead to the teacher having a slightly different view of the situation and being happy to continue.

If specific strategies are identified as having been used before, it is best to question about these with the expectation that they *will* work again.

- How will you do that again?

- How will you use that same idea with Ben?

- As you try out that trick with Billy, what do you think you might notice?

The conversation may finish with a request that the teacher "keep on the lookout for any small signs that Nathan is keeping on showing that he can get his work done" and an agreement to review the situation, or with a comment such as "I'll be back here next Friday and will be really interested in hearing from you how you go using that same strategy with Philip".

Future focused questions may also be useful, although we need to be careful not to appear to be using "fancy techniques".

- Okay, I think I get the picture. Now, before I begin to figure out how to work with a student, I like to be clear about where it is we are heading., since my ideas about what will be a solution to this problem might not be the same as yours — and yours are the important ones. So, just imagine that you are able to change Natalie's behaviour in class, how will we know? What will you and others see differently in her behaviour that will tell you that things have worked?

- I can see that you are prepared to do almost anything to deal with this problem. Tell me, what will be a small sign to you, something that you'll notice in the next week or so, that will tell you that the situation is improving (or that you are handling it better)?

Some teachers will be willing to try out, practice, or even pretend some of the solution-state ideas. This might be framed as an "experiment".

- Look, this might sound crazy, but I wonder if you would be prepared to try an experiment. I know that it is Tom's behaviour that drives you crazy, and he ought to change rather than you having to. Still, maybe you can do something that will have some effect on him. How about, as an experiment, have a go in a couple of lessons this week pretending that things are better — pretending that he isn't a problem any more? I know that seems weird, but it might be very useful to see how he reacts to that.

Asking teachers to "do something different"

Sometimes, teachers will be willing to respond to more direct suggestions from counsellors, although it is preferable that these arise out of some of the kinds of questions outlined above, so they are framed more as teacher and counsellor working out *together* how to proceed.

Teacher and counsellor might then discuss a strategy that involves doing something that is not part of the usual pattern of the problem interaction. This might or might not include an explanation from the counsellor along the lines of "it seems that things are really stuck and what you are doing just isn't working any more, so maybe we need to do something completely different". Doing something different might also be explained as doing something to surprise the student, not giving the student the satisfaction of triggering your usual reaction, and so on.

I remember, when I was in Sixth Form at high school, talking one day to the Deputy in his office about something to do with a student activity we were arranging. As we talked, he was standing near his window, looking out, and suddenly beckoned me to the window. Whilst continuing to talk to me, he pointed down and I could see three well-known third form students smoking behind the building. They were out of sight — or so they thought, however they had not counted on being seen from above. Without stopping our conversation, the Deputy quietly emptied his metal wastepaper bin and filled it with water. He took it to the window, opened the window, and slowly poured the water onto the three smokers below. After shutting the window, he noticed the puzzled look on my face and commented, "I don't know, I'm sick of having those three on detention for smoking and it doesn't seem to make any difference to them anyway. So I thought it was time to try something else."

Only many years alter did I begin to suspect that he must have been a secret brief therapist! The students knew, of course, where the water had come from and were hardly likely to complain. The Deputy had conveyed his message without the usual confrontation that, as he conceded, was not working anyway.

Kral (1989a) gives an example of staff's concern about students' promiscuous behaviour on a couch in a senior students' lounge area, where it became clear that the students were deaf to appeals to reason, morality or discipline. Staff were contemplating imposing more severe penalties, or involving the students' parents, however the school psychologist could see that this was becoming a pattern of teachers doing "more of the same that is not working". He advised them simply, and without any warning or comment, to remove the couch from the lounge and to feign complete ignorance if questioned by the students. Some days later, they were to put the couch back in the lounge, again without any comment. He comments that the behaviour was not a problem after this.

Whenever teachers find themselves stuck or at an impasse with a student or group of students, it is almost always that case that they are continuing to apply sensible, reasonable and well-tried strategies for dealing with the situation — but that these are just not working. Thus, the counsellor's job often amounts to finding ways to get the teachers to *stop* doing what isn't working and/or to do something different.

Many classroom difficulties can be seen in this light and effective intervention can be achieved by finding a small way to encourage the teacher to behave differently. Of course, it helps if the teacher has a sense of humour!

> Kral (1989a) relates another example (which, he says, came from a popular magazine) in which a relief teacher came into a well-known disruptive class and found them in uproar. She realised that she would be wasting her time to try to "shout them down" so walked calmly to the middle of the room, flipped open her hand-mirror and said loudly but determinedly, "Beam me up Scotty, there's no intelligent life here!". The class reportedly settled, in some puzzlement.

13   HELPING SCHOOL STAFF NOTICE DIFFERENCE

The idea of "exceptions" asserts that change is most likely to occur by focussing on what is (already) going right, rather than on trying to change what is going wrong. In the counselling situation, we have already seen that exceptions may provide the "building blocks" of changed behaviour. In other situations, other approaches will be necessary to bring about change in an individual student's behaviour.

However, whatever may or may not happen in a counselling or therapy situation, the fact remains that school staff have certain expectations of students and, once a student has been identified as a "problem", staff are more likely to notice behaviour that confirms that view. This is NOT because they are biased, or malicious, but because it is human nature to notice that which fits with the view we have of things.

I do not want to suggest that teachers' focus on problem behaviour is the REASON for ongoing difficulties. Nonetheless, my experience is that finding ways to encourage teachers to respond to different (that is, non-problem) behaviour can make an enormous difference in the behaviour of the student.

It seems to be human nature that, once we know someone has (or has had) a problem, we are more likely to see evidence of it and less likely to notice anything that is different. Every school student is familiar with the effect of a student gaining a "reputation" within the school. Thirty students may be misbehaving, but it is the one who is "known" as a troublemaker who will be noticed. Therefore, an important way to help students with their reintroduction to school, or their consolidating changes they might have made, is to find ways to encourage such people to notice evidence of change.

Our work with a student does not happen in isolation. If we manage to help a student begin to behave differently at school, it makes sense that the persistence of this new behaviour will be affected by other people's responses. That is, teachers will either notice, and respond to, new behaviour in a way that reinforces it — or, they will be sceptical about change and so will be likely to notice, and respond to, small incidents that suggest lack of change, which fails to reinforce the student's efforts.

Thus, an important part of the counsellor's role is that of finding ways to encourage school staff to notice small changes in a student and respond to these. Unfortunately, a simple request to "look for the positives" is unlikely to be successful once a student has become "known" as a problem. We need to find ways to bring changed behaviour to the attention of teachers, and the school executive, in a way that does not seem to them that we are "manipulating" their view of the situation.

So, we might look for various ways of encouraging school staff to notice difference.

This is not just a matter of "looking for the positives" (in the learning theory sense). Rather, it is a matter of recognising that what we (choose to) notice and respond to actually helps create the "reality" within which a student will behave.

Thus, we might think about any kind of behaviour monitoring (whether it be checklists, data collection, star charts, and so on) in terms of whether they help student and teacher focus on evidence (even small steps) of change — change that might be built upon. I have already discussed the use of "observational tasks" in counselling — tasks that encourage clients simply to look for differences in their own behaviour. Within the school situation, similar tasks might be used and might form the basis for more formal recording.

"Keep data about different behaviour"

I was asked to do an assessment of a girl attending a special unit.

Moderately intellectually handicapped, Tracey had a family history of abuse and neglect and had had periods away from her parents' care. The assessment was requested by the school, who were concerned that she was becoming more and more unmanageable, was requiring constant individual supervision, and was not responding to any normal approaches to discipline.

Tracey's mother, on the other hand, claimed that she had no real difficulties with her. She agreed that she was sometimes a handful however felt that she was generally able to manage this. She could not understand the school's concerns and frustration, saying that she could trust her to walk to the corner shop for her and so did not believe that she required the degree of supervision they claimed. She felt they were "scapegoating" her.

The school, produced detailed evidence of Tracey's behaviour problem. As special educators, they were fond of collecting detailed behavioural data, and had constructed charts and checklists of her behaviour over time, which presented a gloomy picture. Of course, the behavioural data, by its very nature, showed frequency and severity of problem behaviour and did not allow for any indication of successful behaviour. If their protocol did not allow for the recording of nonproblem behaviour, then it followed that they were unlikely even to notice such behaviour. (Equally, one might wonder if mother's "rosy" view made it unlikely that she would notice misbehaviour — and one could see this as "denial", as "minimisation", or simply as a matter of perspective).

I met with the school and listened while the principal and teacher recounted their frustrations. Whatever I might have thought about the substance of their complaints, it was important that they feel heard. If they felt that I was dismissing their concerns, it would follow naturally that they would either not cooperate with any subsequent suggestions, or would be preoccupied with "proving" to me how bad things were. They were clearly concerned that mother was minimising the situation, since they felt she did not want to admit her own incompetence, and wanted me to realise the enormity of the problem.

The school's view was that Tracey required long-term therapy, since they assumed her difficulties were caused by her earlier abuse. They doubted that anything could change without such intensive therapy and, even then, were unsure if the school could continue to tolerate the behaviour in the meantime. Nonetheless, they would be happy to implement any behavioural or other intervention that I might suggest. I spent more than an hour listening to their concerns, and felt this important.

I had a brief meeting with mother. My view was that, if she felt she was managing, it was not my place to try to establish that she was not. Certainly, she dealt with some behaviours in ways that I would have handled differently, however she seemed to be managing and nothing I saw gave me reason to be overly concerned. In fact, I was quite impressed with many of the strategies she employed — most of which stemmed from her view that the behaviour was "naughty" (and so could be controlled) rather than that it was "disturbed".

I followed up my visit to the school with a letter (then a phone call), in which I acknowledged the school's difficulties and thanked them for the detailed information they had provided. I said that I would be devising a behavioural programme, as a first step to getting things under control, and was grateful for their willingness to cooperate with such a programme. I asked if they would be prepared to collect some further data that would assist me in planning this programme.

My request was that the principal, the teacher, and the teacher's aide, keep as detailed observational data as possible of any behaviour that suggested that Tracey was capable of responding, even in small ways, to a behavioural programme. The school personnel were more than happy to go along with this request.

Essentially, this was a request that they look for different kinds of behaviour — that they focus on the positive rather than the negative. However, simply asking them to look for evidence of good behaviour would have been too much at variance with their view and may have antagonised them. It was important that my request be framed in a way that fitted with their perspective. Most teachers are familiar with the notion of focussing on positives, and a request that they do so may make no difference if it does not fit with their broader view of the situation. The collection of detailed behavioural data was an activity that was familiar to them and which they considered important, thus my request was consistent with their way of thinking about their role and just introduced a small difference into their usual practice.

Some weeks later, feeling guilty that I had not yet provided any specific programme, I spoke to the teacher. She dismissed my concern, saying that they had decided that a combined home-school strategy was warranted and that Tracey's mother had agreed to use the same strategies at home that the school employed to manage her behaviour. This, she said, had made an enormous difference and they no longer saw therapy as urgent. When I enquired about the particular strategies, she recounted the same ideas that mother had been using all along!

It did not matter that the school did not acknowledge that these approaches came from Tracey's mother. What was important was that the process of attending to different behaviour had seemed to allow their previously "stuck" view to become more flexible, and they had then been able to find a solution to the situation.

We have used similar ideas in other situations.

For example, when involved with counselling a student, and when it was clear that the school staff hoped that things would work successfully, we have met with staff and said something along the lines of "We can see how frustrating Belinda's behaviour has been and we hope that the counselling we are doing will make a difference. However, it will not happen overnight — changing her longstanding difficulties might take some time. In the meantime, it would be very helpful if you could look out for, and take note of, any behaviour that suggests that Belinda is even beginning to display different behaviour."

Again, such a request needs to fit with the teacher's view of the situation and must not be expressed in such a way as to invalidate the teacher's experience of difficulties. When a request is phrased in a manner that makes sense, and does not imply an overly-optimistic view, most teachers will be happy to look out for behaviours that may be built upon.

The notion of "building on" positive behaviour may in itself be useful. I have sometimes explained to teachers (after making clear that I understood how difficult things had been) that my experience suggested that counselling worked better if it sought to build on those small behaviours that were already happening in the "right" direction. They were usually prepared to look out for these.

Self-monitoring of changed behaviour

Schools often use "behaviour cards" — cards on which the teacher writes a comment about the student at the end of each lesson, which are taken to the Principal at the end of each day and then taken home to be read and signed by parents. Presumably, this procedure reflects an assumption that the constant scrutiny of the student's behaviour provides motivation for him or her to behave differently. The problem with these cards is that they are only used for students who are identified as problems, and teachers all know this. Thus, the very appearance of such a card is virtually a "signal" that this is a troublesome student and so may be an invitation to find something to criticise.

I was concerned that Justin's return to school might be greeted by a search for evidence of failure. Since he was returning from suspension "on probation" for a term, a concentration on looking for misbehaviour would not be helpful. If teachers searched for indications that he was not behaving properly, they would probably find some! I spoke to the school, explaining that part of the emphasis in therapy had been on Justin monitoring his own behaviour and taking responsibility for himself. (We had not used this specific language during therapy; however, it was important in this conversation that I use language that would be meaningful to the school personnel). I asked if the school would be willing to provide opportunities for him to continue these self-monitoring skills. When the school principal agreed that they would be happy to do so, I asked if they would give Justin a set of "behaviour cards" but that these were for Justin to write comments, at the end of each lesson, about his own behaviour. I could sense over the phone the Principal's scepticism about whether Justin would complete this task or how seriously he would take it, and I suspect his plan had been for teachers to monitor Justin's behaviour. Nonetheless, he agreed to give my suggestion a try. I suggested that Justin might show the principal his card at the end of each day and take it home to show his parents.

I had discussed this plan with Justin, since he was concerned that the teachers would be "out to get him." He carried out the task, although his comments about his own behaviour during the first few days were hardly profound and he flippantly wrote very positive remarks about himself. Nonetheless, when he showed the Principal his card, on which he had written comments such as "very well behaved", "model student", "showed great improvement", and so on, the Principal was delighted. The very fact that Justin had carried out the task was "news" to him. After a week or so, when Justin began writing more critical comments about his behaviour ("Talked too much in class," "Did not apply himself this class"), the Principal was even happier. Of course, these comments were exactly the kind that, had they been written by a teacher, would have led to Justin being lectured and perhaps threatened with suspension from school. However, framed in this manner, this exercise encouraged the principal to respond positively to Justin's efforts.

(I have used this example in many workshops.
It has been reproduced in Durrant, 1993, pp. 175–176).

14 HOW we SEE STUDENTS makes a DIFFERENCE

Sometimes, people say that a focus on competence, and "exceptions" is an unrealistic stance. Particularly given the pressures of day-to-day classroom activities, some might think that these ideas amount to viewing troublesome students through "rose-coloured glasses." However, this perspective is not just a "stance". Rose-coloured glasses may sometimes be difficult to find. Nonetheless, the glasses we use actually make a difference.

The way we (choose to) view the students with whom we work may actually affect their behaviour. My assertion is that focusing on competence and strength — since I continue to believe that these actually exist in our clients, no matter how "difficult," "disturbed," or "uncooperative" they may appear — makes a it more likely that I (and, hopefully my clients) will see and respond to these qualities.

Modern physics has grappled with the "wave-particle" duality. Having known that light was composed of waves, Einstein's suggestion that light might better be thought of as particles (photons) was a shocking departure from accepted "reality". Even more shocking was the later idea that familiar particles, electrons, under some circumstances were manifest as waves.

As Davies and Gribbin (1991) explain,

> It is hard to see how something can be both a wave and a particle at the same time, and the discovery of the dual nature of both light and electrons caused a great deal of puzzlement at first. When physicists began to speak of wave-particle duality,

> they meant that an electron ... could manifest either a wave or
> a particle aspect depending on circumstances. ... Experiments
> designed to detect waves always measure the wave aspect of
> the electron; experiments designed to detect particles always
> measure the the particle aspect. (p. 201 & 203)

Hence, in the area of quantum physics, the "nature" of the entities being studied is determined by the process of observation. It does not make sense to talk of either wave-like characteristics or particle-like characteristics as being the "true" nature of light. The nature of light at any time is completely determined by the way the experimenters *choose* to see it, and we can only speculate about what form it takes at other times.

So, what has this to do with our work in schools? It confirms the idea that "reality" (as it relates to the nature of people) is not as clear-cut as our positivist approaches have suggested. It suggests to me that our diagnostic categories, our assessment results, our personality attributions, and so on, are as much products of the process of deriving them as they are characteristics of the student or adult whom we are assessing or describing.

I have summarised elsewhere the implication of this conclusion for the way I view my work:

> Hence, nothing is certain — we have a choice about how
> we wish to view the people with whom we work. We can
> either view them as manifestations of pathology and deficit *or*
> we can view them as representing a degree of competence and
> skill. We cannot do both. *If we choose* to view them in terms of
> pathology, then the focus on problems that this perspective
> requires makes it much more difficult for us to recognize their
> strengths and resources. On the other hand, *if we choose* to
> view them as competent and resourceful, then our focus on
> strengths is more likely to obscure their deficits from our view.
> ... My experience is that, the more I strive (and, some-
> times, struggle) to see my clients as competent and successful
> so the more they tend to demonstrate these characteristics (and,
> at the same time, the more I simply don't notice their deficits
> or pathology). (Durrant, 1993, p. 186)

15   REFERENCES and READING LIST

Since this book is designed to provide a resource for school counsellors and psychologists, the following reference list is divided into three sections.

The "General" references are those referred to in the text, and include essential works in the brief and family therapy field. "Specific applications of brief therapy principles" includes books and articles that illustrate the use of brief therapy ideas in particular contexts, or with particular client populations. "Applications to school problems" are those references which specifically address school problems and school situations.

General

Bateson, G. (1979). *Mind and nature: A necessary unity.* London: Wildwood House.

Bodin, A. M. (1981). "The interactional view: Family therapy approaches of the Mental Research Institute". In A. Gurman & D. Kniskern (Eds.) *Handbook of family therapy.* New York: Brunner/Mazel.

Cade, B. & O'Hanlon, W. H. (1993). *A brief guide to brief therapy.* New York: W. W. Norton.

Davies, P. & Gribbin, J. (1992). *The matter myth: Beyond chaos and complexity.* London: Penguin.

de Shazer, S. (1985). *Keys to solution in brief therapy.* New York: W.W.

Norton.

de Shazer, S. (1988). *Clues: Investigating solutions in brief therapy*. New York: W.W. Norton.

de Shazer, S. (1991). *Putting difference to work*. New York: W.W. Norton.

de Shazer, S., Berg, I. K., Lipchik, E., Nunnally, E., Molnar, A., Gingerich, W. & Weiner-Davis, M. (1986). "Brief therapy: Focused solution development", *Family Process*, 25(2), 207–222.

de Shazer, S. & Molnar, A. (1984). "Four useful interventions in brief family therapy", *Journal of Marital & Family Therapy*, 10(3), 297–304.

Epston, D. (1984). "Guest address", *Australian Journal of Family Therapy*, 5(1), 11–16.

Erickson, M. H. & Rossi, E. L. (1979). *Hypnotherapy: An exploratory casebook*. New York: Irvington Publishers, Inc.

Fisch, R.,Weakland, J. H. & Segal, L. (1982). *The tactics of change: Doing therapy briefly*. San Francisco: Jossey-Bass Publishers.

Furman, B. & Ahola, T. (1992) *Solution talk*. New York: W. W. Norton.

Haley, J. (1973). *Uncommon therapy: The psychiatric techniques of Milton H Erickson*. New York: W.W. Norton.

Kelly, G. (1955). *The psychology of personal constructs*. New York: W. W. Norton.

Kowalski, K. & Kral, R. (1989). "The geometry of solution: Using the scaling technique", *Family Therapy Case Studies*, 4(1), 59–66.

Kral, R. & Kowalski, K. (1989). "After the miracle: The second stage in Solution-Focused Brief Therapy", *Journal of Strategic & Systemic Therapies*, 8(3), 73–76.

Lipchik, E. & de Shazer, S. (1986). "The purposeful interview", Journal of Strategic and Systemic Therapies, 5(1), 88-99.

Lipchik, E. (1988). "Interviewing with a constructive ear", *Dulwich Centre Newsletter*, Winter, 3-7.

Lipchik, E. (1988). "Purposeful sequences for beginning the solution-focused interview", In E. Lipchik, (Ed.), *Interviewing*. Rockville, MA: Aspen.

Lipchik, E. (1993). "A reflecting interview", *Journal of Strategic & Systemic Therapies*, 11(4), 59–74.

Lustig, H. (1975). *The artistry of Milton Erickson*. Videotape, Ardmore, PA.

O'Hanlon, W. H. (1987). *Taproots: Underlying principles of Milton H Erickson's therapy and hypnosis*. New York: W.W. Norton.

O'Hanlon, W. H. & Hexum, A. L. (1990). *An uncommon casebook: The complete clinical work of Milton H. Erickson, M. D.* New York: W. W. Norton.

O'Hanlon, B. & Wilk, J. (1987). *Shifting contexts: The generation of effective psychotherapy*. New York:Guilford Press.

O'Hanlon, W. H. & Weiner-Davis, M. (1989). In Search of Solutions: A New Direction in Psychotherapy. New York: W.W. Norton.

Penn, P. (1985) "'Feed-forward: Future questions, future maps", *Family Process*, 24, 299–311.

Rosen, S. (1982). *My voice will go with you: The teaching tales of Milton H. Erickson, M. D.* New York: W. W. Norton.

Rossi, E. (1980). *The collected papers of Milton Erickson*. New York: Irvington Publishers, Inc.

Simon, R. (1983). "Erickson's way", *The Family Therapy Networker*, (September-October), 21-27.

Talmon, M. (1990). *Single session therapy*. San Francisco: Jossey-Bass..

Tomm, K. (1987) 'Interventive interviewing', *Family Process*, 26, 167–183.

Walter, J. & Peller, J. (1992). *Becoming solution focused in brief therapy*. New York: Brunner/Mazel.

Watzlawick, P.,Weakland, J. & Fisch, R. (1974). *Change : Principles of problem formation and problem resolution*. NY: W. W. Norton.

Weakland, J. H., Fisch, R.,Watzlawick, P. & Bodin, A. (1974). "Brief therapy: Focused problem resolution", *Family Process*, 13, 141–168.

Weiner-Davies, M.,de Shazer, S. & Gingerich, W. J. (1987). "Building on pretreatment change to construct the therapeutic solution: An exploratory study", *Journal of Marital and Family Therapy*, 13, 359-363.

Weinhaus, E. & Friedman, K. (1987). *Stop struggling with your teenager.* Ringwood, Vic.: McPhee Gribble / Penguin.

White, M. (1988). "The externalizing of the problem and the re-authoring of lives and relationships", *Dulwich Centre Newsletter,* Summer, 3-21.

White, M. & Epston, D. (1989). *Literate means to therapeutic ends.* Adelaide: Dulwich Centre Publications.

Zukav, G. (1979). *The Dancing Wu-Li Masters.* London: Fontana.

Specific applications of brief therapy principles

Berg, K. (1991). *Family Preservation: A Brief therapy workbook.* London: B T Press.

Berg, I. K. & Miller, S. (1992). *Working with the problem drinker: A solution-focused approach.* New York: W. W. Norton.

Blymer, D. & Smith, C. (1992). "Utilization of detoxification: A brief, solution-oriented treatment approach for chemical dependency", *Family Therapy Case Studies,* 6(2), 53–62.

Cade, B. (1988). "The art of neglecting children: Passing the responsibility back", *Family Therapy Case Studies,* 3(2), 27–34.

Cade, B. (1989). "Over-responsibility and under-responsibility: Opposite sides of the coin", A celebration of family therapy — 10th anniversary issue of *The Journal of Family Therapy,* Spring, 103–121.

Cade, B. (1990). "The mini-tornado: Turning "hyperactivity" into energy", *Family Therapy Case Studies,* 5(1), 45-50.

Dolan, Y. (1991). *Resolving sexual abuse: Solution-focused therapy and Ericksonian hypnosis for adult survivors.* New York: W. W. Norton.

Durrant, M. (1993) *Residential treatment: A cooperative competency-based approach to therapy and program design.* New York: W. W. Norton.

Durrant, M. (1990). "Saying 'boo' to Mr Scarey: Writing a book provides a solution", *Family Therapy Case Studies,* 5(1), 39–44.

Durrant, M. (1989). "Scaring fears: Making exceptions to problem behaviour meaningful", *Family Therapy Case Studies,* 4(2), 15–31.

Durrant, M. (1987). "Therapy with young people who have been victims of sexual assault", *Family Therapy Case Studies*, 2(1), 57–63.

Durrant, M. & Coles, D. (1990). "Michael White's cybernetic approach". In T. Todd & M. Selekman (Eds.), *Family therapy approaches with adolescent substance abusers* (pp. 135-175). Boston: Allyn & Bacon.

Durrant, M. & Kowalski, K. (1990). "Overcoming the effects of sexual abuse: Developing a self-perception of competence". In M. Durrant & C. White (Eds.), *Ideas for therapy with sexual abuse* (pp. 65-110). Adelaide: Dulwich Centre Publications.

Durrant, M. & Kowalski, K. (1993) 'Enhancing views of competence', Chapter in S. Friedman (Ed.) *The new language of change: Constructive collaboration in psychotherapy.* New York: Guilford.

Durrant, M. & White, C. (Eds.). (1990). *Ideas for therapy with sexual abuse.* Adelaide: Dulwich Centre Publications.

Hudson, P. & O'Hanlon, W. (1992) *Rewriting love stories.* New York: W. W. Norton.

Molnar, A. & de Shazer, S. (1987). "Solution focused therapy: Toward the identification of therapeutic tasks", *Journal of Marital & Family Therapy*, 13(4), 349–358.

Selekman, M. (1991). "The solution-oriented parenting group", *Journal of strategic & systemic therapies*, 10(1), 36–49.

Tiggeman, J. & Smith, G. (1989). "Adolescent "shock therapy": Teenagers shocking their critics", *Dulwich Centre Newsletter*(Winter).

Weakland, J. & Jordan, L. (1990). "Working briefly with reluctant clients: Child protective services as an example", *Family Therapy Case Studies*, 5(2), 51-68.

Applications to school problems

Amatea, E. S. (1989). *Brief strategic intervention for school problems.* San Francisco: Jossey-Bass.

Brown, J. (1986). "The pretend technique: An intervention in the teacher-student system", *Family Therapy Case Studies*, 1(2), 13–15.

Craig, R. (1987). "News that made a difference: Teamwork on a serious problem in a school context", *Family Therapy Case Studies*, 2, 5–14.

Kowalski, K. (1990). "The girl with the know-how: Finding solutions to a school problem", *Family Therapy Case Studies*, 5(1), 3–14.

Kral, R. (1986). "Indirect therapy in the schools", in S. de Shazer & R. Kral (Eds.). *Indirect approaches in therapy*. Rockville, MA: Aspen.

Kral, R. (1988). "A quick little step: The "5 'D' process" for Solution Focused Brief Therapy", *Family Therapy Case Studies*, 3(1), 13-17.

Kral, R. (1989a). *Strategies that work: Techniques for solution in the schools*. Milwaukee, WI: Brief Family Therapy Center.

Kral, R. (1989b). "The Q. I. K. (Quick Interview for Kids): Psychodiagnostics for teens and children - brief therapy style", *Family Therapy Case Studies*, 4(2), 61-65.

Lindquist, B., Molnar, A. & Brauchmann, L. (1987). "Working with school related problems without going to school: Considerations for systemic practice", *Jnl of Strategic and Systemic Therapies*, 6, 44-50.

Molnar, A. & Lindquist, B. (1989). *Changing problem behavior in schools*. San Francisco: Jossey-Bass Publishers.

Murphy, J. (1992). "Brief strategic family intervention for school-related problems", *Family Therapy Case Studies*, 7(1), 59–71

Stewart, B. & Nodrick, B. (1990) "The learning disabled lifestyle: From reification to liberation", *Family Therapy Case Studies*, 5(1), 61–74.

White, L. J., Summerlin, M. L., Loos, V. E. & Epstein, E. S. (1992). "School and family consultation: A language-systems approach". In M. Fine & C. Carlson (Eds.), *The handbook of family-school intervention: A systems perspective*". Boston, MA.: Allyn & Bacon.